the

PIRATE'S
guide to
S▲LES

A Seller's Guide for
Getting from Why to Buy

——TYLER MENKE ——

DEDICATION

In memory of my father.

Life on the Vine

By Tyler Menke

Loved by many,
It's easy to see.
How the seeds you planted,
grew inside of me.
Left this earth,
different than before.
Lost the fight,
but won for us the war.

Memories live on,
months and years to come.
Lessons taught,
passed from Dad to Son.
Reaching out,
spreading wide and far,
My guiding light,
every wish upon a star.

Richard Clarence Menke

5/4/59 - 5/6/19

CONTENTS PART ONE

THE PIRATE'S GUIDE TO SALES

CONTENTS PART TWO

ACKNOWLEDGMENTS

There are many people to thank for helping bring this dream to life. First and foremost, I'd like to thank my family and friends. My wife, Michelle, is my rock, and my three kids teach me as much as I teach them, if not more!

I also would like to thank Rod Colvin of Addicus Books for coaching me in the early stages and Peter Shankman for his inspiration and guidance. In addition, there were many who were generous with their time in helping either read the early versions for feedback or in contributing tips and tricks from their sales careers. With hope, I'm not forgetting any names—I'd like to thank Aaron Wozniak, Ryan Zimmer, Bryan Sackmann, Rocky Baker, Amanda Anglin, Will Krieger, Nick Fasulo, Heather Bressler, Lori Werner, Bryan Smith, Greg Thomas, Lynzee Mendenhall, Jake Andreadis, Andrew Koehler, Bryan McDonald, and Brian Menke. Lastly, I'd like to give a special shout out to my editor, Greg Brown, who fixed all my grammar mistakes and tightened up my prose.

AUTHOR'S PREFACE

No one likes to be sold, but people generally like to buy. What is with that? We buy things all the time we never thought we needed and often with little reflection on the process. Yet, everyone remembers the car purchase or the cell phone mall pitch that left you "hating" salespeople. Selling shouldn't leave you or the customer feeling "sleazy" or "had." Sure, this may work with one-time purchases, but in today's world, it's far too expensive and competitive to acquire new customers each and every time. A truth of sales: *sustainability thrives and dies with the lifetime customer.* Many believe the best way to achieve long-term success is to spend more time on the story and invite the customer to join us on the journey.

Whether you're a CEO, salesperson, business owner, or freelancer, getting your message across is paramount. Of course, in addition to this being an important skill, selling is often the cause of failed products and businesses. There are countless examples of good products and good salespeople that failed to achieve the level of success deserved.

If you've been around sales for a while, you may have noticed a shift in the way people are selling. Gone are the days of relationship-building and questioning people to death with "spin selling" (sorry Neil Rackham). Today's selling is all about the story and providing value. No longer can we simply prepare, plan, and pitch our way to success.

According to leading marketing firms, we are exposed to an average of four to six thousand ads every day. We have become very sensitive to responding, or even listening, to anything that sounds remotely like a sales pitch.

So how do you get someone to buy something and have them feel good about it? Experts agree it's in the message and that it takes a lot of research and planning on the part of the seller to understand the buyer. This all leads to the ever important and frequently referenced WHY. It's a three-letter word so powerful that it has led many to devote their entire careers to understanding it, and yet it's too often analyzed in hindsight. Think about it. Detectives start with "the why" in trying to solve murders. Hostage negotiators seek to learn about "the why" in attempting to come to terms of release. And all over the world counselors are getting paid to ask poignant questions about "the why" in an attempt to understand patients. We all struggle every day to understand our own WHY, but we rarely spend any time at all understanding the whys of others.

The art of story selling is to uncover the why. Then and only then do you craft a concise, memorable, and emotionally gripping message that gets people to buy. This book aims to provide a framework for doing so in a series of skill sets analyzed through the eyes of researchers, top performing salespeople, and behavioral psychologists. We would like you to think of it as a "pirate's guide" because, like the late Steve Jobs once said, "it's more fun to be a pirate than to join the navy." All of us have had classic sales tactics entrenched in our brains, and some of those tactics have applications in today's business world. However, the true innovators and leaders seek to understand before being understood; and thus, we can't simply ignore the progress being made elsewhere. We must go out and find it, understand it, pirate it, and make it our own. We hope this book helps you do just that!

INTRODUCTION

PREPARE FOR THE VOYAGE

If the "why" is so important then I'd be a hypocrite to not start with why I'm writing this book. The answer is simple. I am a salesman. It used to pain me to say that, and in fact I still cringed a little typing it. The reason for this? Well, like most people, I have been "sold" far too many times and have become sensitive to anyone stealing my time with disingenuous attempts to line their pockets or boost their ego at my expense.

However, what I've learned the past twelve years selling medical devices, genetic testing, and ocean and air freight forwarding services is that you can be successful in sales and feel good about it at the same time. In addition, most sales books I've encountered aren't even written by salespeople. If they are, they often fail to combine both human psychology and real-world learnings. This book aims to combine both real world perspectives from top salespeople and knowledge from leading experts in human behavior. You will learn tips from CIA hostage negotiators, top sales professionals, human behavioral psychologists, and, yes, even input from some of the sales books you have read or should read. It's a pirate's guide because while the years of experience and research are my own, a lot is to be learned by all the experts out there. With hope this book will help shorten the path that has now taken me more than a decade of analysis to organize.

How This Book Is Organized

One of the more life-changing books I've read is *Unlimited Memory* by Kevin Horsley. In his book, Horsley debunks the mythical "photographic" memory. It doesn't exist, or at least not in the way we think it does. People that memorize entire encyclopedias of information do so with a system. It's a system that can be learned and works for everyone. The trick is in organizing information and storing it in places in your mind that you can visualize and follow.

For example, numbers are nearly impossible for people to remember because individually they mean nothing. However, he teaches you to turn each number into a letter and form words. Once you learn that M (looks like a 3 on its side) and T (makes a one with the down stroke of your pen) then you would know the word TOMATO is 131 (vowels have no value and are used to make your own words out of numbers). Learn the system, use creativity to make a visual (like cutting a tomato with your credit card), and now you know the security code on the back of my visa!

Using this principle, this book is organized in a similar way so that the concepts will stick. In Part One, *Preparing for the Voyage*, each of the eight concepts correlate with parts of a pirate ship. Don't worry—you don't have to be a ship expert to know or remember this.

We'll start by getting organized and naming our ship, beginning with a planning strategy that will tidy up your trunk and tighten up your personal brand. Then we will plot our destination and waypoints as we begin to formulate our goals, both short and long term. From there we will learn more about our fellow man from the likes of Ray Dalio, Dale Carnegie, and even Mark Manson, as we start to assemble our crew and learn to lead like a captain. Once settled in, we will finally pull anchor. Chapter six is all about uncovering the why. This is the part you often can't see, the underside of the boat, so to speak, which you simply can't move on without dragging out. From there we will use a map to plan, a compass to prospect, and even learn targeting from a world class surfer in *The Cannonball Strategy*. Part one and voyage prep will then culminate with decision making strategy using both your systems, the sails and the oars, as we learn how to think fast and slow from acclaimed Nobel Prize winner Daniel Kahneman.

Part Two of the book, *The Points of Sail,* frames up the sale itself. We will discuss six steps from opening to close and cover all points in between. In addition to continued education and advice from the top business minds and behavioral phycologists around the country, you will also get firsthand examples and practical application of these steps from leading sales reps. Combined, the four interviewed selling professionals have amassed an astounding 30 President's Club wins! You'll even learn tactile negotiation from ex-CIA hostage negotiators. From there, we will steer the story and lessons to a close, before ending the whole shebang in a riveting old pirate tale in the "burning of the boats!"

Prepare for a journey and a lot of great stories. This will not be your average boring business book with lessons and formulas. While practical application will be necessary and available in the companion guide, the stories, tips, and tricks relayed along the way are sure to sharpen anyone's selling game.

The Mind Map

Before we get started, briefly study the mind map below.

Preparing to Sail

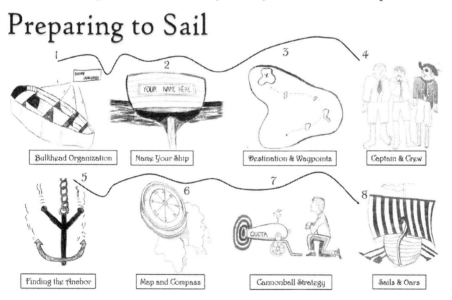

| 1 Bulkhead Organization | 2 Name Your Ship | 3 Destination & Waypoints | 4 Captain & Crew |
| 5 Finding the Anchor | 6 Map and Compass | 7 Cannonball Strategy | 8 Sails & Oars |

In short, what we have here is a visual representation of the journey we're about to embark on, and the journey you'll embark on, along the path towards more effective selling.

Picture starting off by outfitting your boat and organizing the bulkhead. Then imagine yourself naming your maiden voyage and painting the ship's name in white across the bow of the boat. From there, begin to organize and assemble your thoughts and the needed tools and crew members. Then store them on your boat. Once ready, draw a picture in your mind that depicts you dragging a Y-shaped anchor from the bottom of the ocean floor. Really envision the effort needed to lift it, and the weight it carries. The anchor will become analogous to the uncovering of the innermost influence and opportunities within your customer base.

Ask yourself what tools will be needed along the way in order to travel and navigate? Might you use a map to plan and a compass when out prospecting? Picture the map as more of your guide, and the compass as navigation of the points in between. This is how you will structure your route. Picture all tools as necessary and essential carry-on luggage and bring them with you.

Lastly, envision yourself approaching your first targets at sea. You will begin approaching quickly, with sails full mast, before slowing your speed and resorting to an oar-only model as you draw near. These are your decision-making systems, and like both sides of the brain, you'll need to learn how and when you use both.

As you approach your first bountiful boats of booty, begin to sight in your cannon. Imagine yourself then striking a match and firing a massive cannonball through the air and into the side of your target.

Once you've done this, you've then recounted and remembered the eight steps of selling preparation: goal setting, self-analysis, organization, finding the why, customer behavior analysis, planning and prospecting, targeting, and decision making.

Six Points of Sail

While all the concepts in Part One of the book cover parts or items on the boat, Part Two is where we take action. Each of the six points of sail correlate with the sailing the pirates themselves did. Start by picturing yourself climbing over the rail and taking hold of the helm. Feel the wheel as you grab ahold and begin to take control of the sale and ship itself.

Next up on the voyage is scouting a new view in an effort to cast a perspective on the future. For that, imagine climbing to the top of a giant crow's nest and looking out over the ocean ahead, viewing the horizon from the highest point. What can you see now that you couldn't from down below?

Once you've done so, quickly climb back down because you have real work awaiting you. Start by taking control and shifting perspective. But remember: the boats aren't going to move until you lift anchor and get wind in your sails.

Then, to pick up speed, try to find an underwater current to ride that will guide you effortlessly through the ocean channels. How valuable are these times at sea where you move with so little effort?

Now for the tricky part. Imagine you are so close to delivering on a huge shipment of loot and gold, but your recent charades have found you teetering on the outer end of a long wooden plank. Success is now between you and the hands that put you there, and the shift of power is not in your favor. How can you negotiate yourself off the ledge and back to safety?

Do so correctly, and you have a pile of gold waiting for you back inside the ship. Get there and you are a hero. Fail and you fall victim with nothing to show for it. These are the six points of sale: *Take the Helm, View the Crow's Nest, Get Wind in Your Sails, Follow the Currents, Walk the Plank, and Deliver the Gold.* And, yes, as you might have guessed, all of them are anchored in the why!

Points of Sail

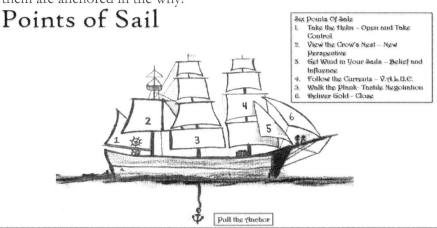

Six Points Of Sale
1. Take the Helm – Open and Take Control
2. View the Crow's Nest – New Perspective
3. Get Wind in Your Sails – Belief and Influence
4. Follow the Currents – V.A.L.U.E.
5. Walk the Plank– Tactile Negotiation
6. Deliver Gold - Close

Pull the Anchor

CHAPTER
One

THE VOYAGE AHEAD

The Art of Story Selling

Growing up on a farm in the city and attending private school was tough at times. Farm life is much different than city life, and you often don't realize this until it's validated by a city person. As kids we all played barefoot in the creeks. We used to shoot blackbirds out of grandma's garden and get a quarter for every confirmed death. We blew up frogs with firecrackers. My brother and I once had a part-time job each summer burying the local vet's animals that had been put down. Weird, right? But hey, it was good money, and we created our own little pet cemetery with headstones and all. Normal kid's stuff (I think not).

Well, as you go through school, you often start getting the question. What do you want to be when you grow up? They like to tie this to your interests. For instance, little Mikey likes math and creating things. Perfect! Mikey will be an engineer. Susy likes to do pretend check-ups on her little brother and stuffed animals. She wants to grow up to be just like her mom and be a doctor! Well, you can imagine then, the career choices they would pick for my charades. The only reasonable choice for a blackbird mercenary, dog burying, frog bomber? You guessed it…a serial killer.

As it turns out, I'm not a serial killer, though I do have a fascination for all the Netflix documentaries on Bundy and Kaczynski. Today, I'm a salesperson working in the medical industry. Lucky for my teachers, and the rest of the world, that crazy stuff we did as kids just taught me to be resourceful and think differently. Sales requires you to think differently and to be authentic. While it might be a good idea for me to hide some of my past stories, they did in fact make me the way I am today. And, well, different sometimes wins the day.

Let me give you an example. My job requires a good bit of travel. There's an old saying that "you can take the kid from the farm, but you can't take the farm out of the kid." One day while boarding a flight this proved true when I was abruptly stopped at security. As it turned out, I had failed to remove a much-too-large pocketknife from my carry on. After a quick strip search, body scan, and knife confiscation, I raced to the plane. It was one of those moments where they were closing the door as I entered to rolling eyes. I skulked into my seat, still short of breath. As I sat down, I stared out the window, trying my hardest to avoid eye contact with annoyed passengers, and it was then I noticed something. In the not-too-distant, far corner of the runway stood a ten-point deer. It was late fall and "because of the farm in me," I knew it was hunting season. "You got to be kidding me?" I thought. "I'm sitting here feeling embarrassed and ashamed for failing to take a pocketknife from my bag and this buck is right by the plane undetected. What a smart son of a bitch." Here was a buck that with the hop of a fence could escape all threat, and we humans board planes feeling safe because of the security *in* the airport? If a deer could get on the runway, then what was to stop a human from gaining access outside and posing a threat to passengers?

After 9/11, air travel forever changed. Why? Because we are reactive as a society, and we had to do something. The challenge is that most criminals think differently and look for easier paths. In fact, were they not criminals, most would probably make great professions for themselves with different choices. Selling and business is about thinking differently and finding ways when others can't. When combined with innovation and a creative narrative, planning and preparation can change people's lives. Doing what everyone else does without at least looking for a better way to message your idea won't get you very far. The trick is to embrace different thoughts and ideas, visualize the outcome, and craft a message that sticks!

Throughout this book, we will continually come back to this concept. There will be lots of stories—because, well, they help connect to the message—but additionally you'll learn a lot of innovative, creative, and proven tactics, all pirated from the best and executed to perfection!

So, stories sell. At this point in human history we all know that. Chip and Dan Heath are two leading experts in the arena of story selling and authors of *Made to Stick*. If you haven't read their book, I strongly recommend you check it out! Until then, let's begin with five tips loosely based on their work.

Develop Your Hook

This is the most important step in selling because if you can't get people to pay attention, then what good is the rest? One of the best ways to achieve this is by doing the *unexpected*. Imagine if you started your next pitch by saying you "hate salespeople and never wanted to be one, until you realized it can be done successfully without doing all the things you used to hate." At the very least, you got the attention of your audience and invited them to learn about where this is heading. The hook is your opening. Done properly, it not only grants you access to proceed but allows you to take control of the helm. The goal is to build immediate credibility and trust. More on this later.

Make It Memorable

Our memory is strongly tied to "visuals," so the key to having your message remembered is to use something simple and visual. Strip your message down to its authentic, bare bones core. Then deliver it with a visual. What is the key differentiator? Every product and company needs a "special sauce". How can you use a visual to demonstrate that benefit or difference? In *Made to Stick*, Chip Heath uses Velcro as a visual example of memory. "If you look at Velcro really close, you will see that one side is all loops, and the other side all hooks," he writes. "The more hooks you secure, the better it sticks." Now that's a visual.

Be Authentic

Trust is so essential to selling that if you never gain it, or worse yet you lose it, you're toast. Here authenticity is often synonymous with agreeability as well. You want at least the majority of your customer base to be able to agree and relate with what you are saying. This, however, must also be genuine. Pretending you understand the customer's world without having experienced it, or with no knowledge of it, will only cause your authenticity to come across as disingenuous. Do your research. When possible, even try to experience what the customer does. By putting yourself in his or her shoes and really feeling the emotions he or she feels in relationship to a product, service, or experience, you'll reach an authentic place of learning.

Elicit Emotion

The goal is to make sure they care and believe. First, identify the emotion that fits your product. Then decide on the vehicle for delivering that feeling. Do you want customers to feel "hope" and that they "can make a difference," or do you want them to feel "inspired" and "motivated"? Should they feel "unique" and "special," or "safe" and "protected"? With these descriptions alone if you were asked to guess the brand behind the feeling could you not conjure up a list of probable prospects? As soon as you hear "inspired," brands like Apple, Ted Talks, and Tesla come to mind. This is because powerful brands understand that emotion drives connection, and connection drives brand loyalty. So, ask yourself, "if I were to separate my product from its message, could my customers identify the name of my company or product from the message alone?" If not, then you haven't made the emotional connection required to be remembered.

Call for Action

Get your customers wanting to take the next step. Like the teaser clips at the end of a great episode of your favorite show, how are you going to get them to take the action you want them to? And most importantly, how can you make that action EASY! One click, one signature, no money down, free installation, trial periods, on and on. There are lots of ways to make it actionable and easy, but ask yourself: if you were the customer, would you act on this?

Putting It All Together

Let's look at the plane story above as an example. It starts with the background and anecdotal info of my upbringing on the farm. By combining authenticity, and I might even add vulnerability, the reader at the very least should be wondering where this story is leading. On an emotional level, most, if not all of us, can relate to a time when we either felt different or uncomfortable. Many have likely even experienced the airport mad dash themselves or had items thrown out that didn't meet TSA standards. Add in the imagery of me sweating my way through security, and of the deer on the runway, and some might even be able to picture the experience. If I was trying to use this story to frame up a new way to handle TSA security, or if I was trying to use it to sell new technology to the airport to secure it from the outside, it might land well and be highly relatable. With a hook, visuals, authenticity, and an emotional connection, the stage has been set for a call to action. So, when will the airports beef up security outside the airport?

CHAPTER
Two

OUTFITTING THE SHIP

Organization in an ADHD Mindset

Now that we've covered how this book is organized, touched on the voyage ahead, and demonstrated the power of a story in selling, it's time to get ourselves in order. I don't mean to sound stereotypical here, but that is a risk, and while what I'm about to say certainly doesn't apply to every salesperson, let's be honest here: most of you reading this book who chose sales as a career have a bit of ADHD. Before you take offense to that, let me tell you that I myself am the recipient of the gift that is the ADHD brain.

I didn't always see it as a gift, though. Having struggled mightily through school to get average grades, it wasn't until I was 28 years old when I was diagnosed. In fact, at 28, when I figured it out, I'd already finished my MBA and was well on my way in my sales career. The realization forever changed my life.

Having just left a two-week training course where I had to remember hundreds of new medical terms and pass a test, I again found myself frustrated. Why did I seemingly have so much more trouble learning than other people? Why couldn't I focus at times? How come in some instances I could learn a new topic or skill in half the time of others, while other instances took me twice as long?

Luckily for me the age-old "better late than never" adage came into play in a primary care appointment the Monday following my training. "Hey doc, so I wanted to ask you something," I said. "Yes, I'm healthy, but something is in fact bugging me. I just spent two weeks in training at work, and I find myself exhausted because I stayed up most nights reviewing and re-reviewing content I needed to learn. My whole life I've struggled to maintain focus for any length of time."

"Have you ever been tested for ADHD?" he asked.

"No," I explained, "but I'm not a hyper person. I thought ADHD was something that only hyper kids have?"

He went on to explain that the DSM (Diagnostic and Statistical Manual used in mental health evaluation) had recently made changes to the terms ADD and ADHD. This was done because it seemed to be treated effectively in much the same way and because it manifested similarly. "For some the 'hyper' is more in the brain and less in outward physical activity," he said. He told me that he himself wasn't diagnosed until adulthood and that it had changed his life in innumerable ways.

After listening to his heartfelt spiel and answering yes to a number of questions that seemingly described me, I decided to take the test. I was diagnosed with ADHD and put on a low dose medication to see if it made a difference. Having already learned good coping skills through a lifetime of trial and error, the addition of this medication turned my brain on like a light switch. All of a sudden, and with little effort, I could learn subject matter, skills, and info in half the time. Not only that, but I could seemingly complete nearly any task in half the time as well. For the first time, I felt, dare I say it, cognitively normal.

Having gone most of my life up to this point thinking I just wasn't that smart; I began to rethink and relearn everything. I even decided to take the Stanford-Binet intelligence test and surprised myself with a 131 IQ result. It was one of those moments where I felt both frustrated and elated. I was frustrated that it had taken me so long to figure this out and elated that, well, I at least finally figured it out. Or at least I thought I had.

Over the next several years, I began to read book after book, learning from anything and everything I could get my hands on. That was until one day I stumbled across a book that would again change my life: *Faster than Normal* by the author and entrepreneur Peter Shankman.

Having ADHD himself hadn't seemed to stop Peter from excelling at his life and his career. He has founded and sold multiple companies, appeared on TEDx and multiple national media platforms, authored several best-selling books, and runs a podcast and website to help others with ADHD. As Peter explains it in his book, "having ADHD is a gift, you just have to know how to use it." His book is a non-scientific, practical approach to living with ADHD and is full of advice for those with and without it. Building on Shankman's work, and using the acronym itself, ADHD, to help aid in the memory of these four practical approaches, we are going to cover: Adjustments to Make (Avast Ye), Dealing with Down Time (Dead Seas), Helpful Tips for Staying the Course (Hornswoggle), and Disruptive Habits to Stop (Dance the Deadman's Jig).

A quick disclaimer: Whether you have ADHD is irrelevant going forward. So, don't worry about the harsh stereotypes of salespeople being a little bit ADHD. If you in fact have ADHD or think you might, then I strongly suggest listening to Peter's podcast and reading his book, in addition to talking to your doctor, but for the purposes of this chapter, we'll spend time on concepts that should help everyone.

A: Adjustments to Make – Avast Ye ("Stop You! Pay Attention")

There are several adjustments that need to be made to get organized. Full disclosure this continues to be a work in progress for me so don't for a second think that I, myself, have all this down. However, these are adjustments I've begun to make, have seen huge results from, and continue to work at.

Wake Up Early

Morning routines have been discussed a lot lately by entrepreneurs and salespeople alike. I get up between 4:30 and 5:30 on most days now and this is coming from a habitually late sleeper. The trick is to start your day right and set the course for productivity. This way, by the time you reach bedtime you're so tired (in a good way) that you fall right asleep. Slowly you will begin to find yourself waking up with no alarm and feeling more rested than ever. Build your own morning routine, but don't do it without a good breakfast. Studies show that eating a good high-protein, nutrient-rich breakfast is vitally important. Your brain needs good sleep and good nutrition to work at its fullest potential.

Mindfulness and Journaling

Spend some time in the early morning hours in mindfulness, either through meditation or journaling. It doesn't have to be a lot of time, but you'll find if you write down or sort through anxiety and push it out of your mind, your day shines through. It's a tough task at first. In fact, you likely won't see the benefits initially. They say it takes a few days or even weeks for people to start rewiring their brain towards positivity, so try to stick with it. It took me about a month before I started to finally understand what all the glowing reviews on mindfulness and mediation were about. And, I say finally because I'd given up many times before. Luckily for me I found tools this time around that helped me stick with it. Apps like Calm and Insight Timer will alert you at set times of the day and break down the sessions into short and attainable chunks. In the beginning, if you're anything like me, two minutes of silence might seem too long. However, over time you learn to appreciate and even enjoy the stillness of your mind. There is a great quote from a well-known business consultant and motivational speaker named Matthew Kelly, that reads "you can learn more from an hour of silence than a year of reading books."

Preparing for the Day and Exercising

After breakfast and journaling, spend some time preparing for your day. Then, if time allows, do some physical exercise or try to do something creative. It doesn't take much physical exercise or brain exercise to build dopamine and endorphins that can be used like a reserve throughout the day. Try it for a week and make your morning routine your own. If it works for you and you'd like to share it with me, I'd love to hear from you. Email me at tyler@thepirateguides.com and tell me what you are doing. I'd love to try it myself and share it with others (this is also something Peter implores one to do as well).

D: Dealing with Down Time – Dead Seas

Down time for salespeople is what the dead seas and winds must have been to the sailors and pirates. As your mother or grandmother probably said, "the idle mind is the devil's playground." Ever notice how the free time that sometimes comes at inexplicable hours of the day seems to lead to anxiety? For salespeople, I think this is a symptom of not having a plan for what to do with that time. We all feel like we should be doing something, but what? The dead air of the day is not a time to pull your sales numbers, particularly if they are bad. It's not the time to fret over cancelled appointments or lost opportunities, either. None of this stuff is remotely productive, and it'll bleed into your work when you do in fact get busy again.

Instead, during down time, planned or otherwise, do something positive and productive. Schedule key appointments or assemble metrics and data that can be shared in a positive way with other customers. Read up on new topics or subject matter related to your field. Whatever it is you choose, pick something that will improve you not diffuse you.

The fact is appointments cancel, and all salespeople go through periods of staleness. Use these periods to reorganize your trunk, your office, or your calendar. Ask yourself, am I going to allow myself this time for my benefit or am I going to use it in unproductive ways and feel crappy afterwards? Studies show that the number-one way to break a bad habit is to think about the negative aspects of the outcome of the choice. How will you feel after you do whatever it is you're going to do with this free time?

H: Helping Stay Course – Hornswoggle (What Pirate's Call Cheap Tricks)

Much like navigation systems today, and the maps of old, tools generally help you stay the course most effectively. In today's world there are more tools than ever before to help with this. Pick a tech ecosystem and stick with it. If it's Google, then learn how to use Drive, Hangouts, Google

Calendar, Google Sheets, Analytics, etc. The benefit: since all the tools are built from one platform, they link together, shortening the learning curve with each application. Having all your messaging, calendar, data, and the like, in separate places is more work than is necessarily needed. Each time you decide to use a new tool for productivity outside of your ecosystem of choice, you lose precious time.

Also, try to separate work and social platforms in regard to time. If you're like me, you might start a project, get a text, check Instagram, and waste an hour before you realized you actually *had* down time. Bucket your time in allotted chucks and try to avoid doing things in conjunction with one another.

D: Disruptive Habits to Stop – Don't Dance the Deadman's Jig

While there are a number of disruptive habits we could all stop, there are a few that seem to plague us all. The first is negative self-talk. I've never met a group of more confident people than salespeople; yet behind those eyeballs, there at times resides a snowball of self-defeat. The snowball starts with one small thing, gets pushed down the hill, and grows with each and every roll. Our minds are like that tiny thread hanging from the seam of a newly pressed suit. Instead of cutting the thread at the source, we instead instinctively pull it. With each pull, and failed attempt to make scissors out of our fingers, the seam unravels and spreads. Before you know it you're left standing with a pant leg separated from the inseam and draped around your ankle.

Don't do this! Instead, when the negative self-talk begins, you need to recognize it, own it, and then do something else. Call a friend/peer in your field or put down your work and fill in with something more productive. Whatever the negative element is, you need to recognize the impact it's having on you. We all have fears, doubts, and insecurities, and on the proverbial roller coaster of the sales cycle, we all have peaks and valleys. Call someone you think might be riding a high or a close friend or relative.

What I've begun to do in times like this is to try to find a video, podcast, or article that puts things back in perspective. It might be a graduation speech, a dying man's last words (I love Jim Valvano's speech from the ESPYs), or something more lighthearted like a Ted Talk on a new topic. Whatever it is, pick something that takes your mind off the snowball and puts it onto something that matters in life.

Obsessing Over Your Sales Numbers

Obsessing over your sales numbers is the second disruptive habit to stop now. When you're at the top of the sales ranks, you can spend tons of wasted time trying to analyze what sales are needed to get you to move further or maintain your position. When you're at the bottom, you will again spend time analyzing how you got there and what sales are needed to move up. There is nothing productive about this. You can boost your confidence in yourself and benchmark yourself. Any time spent reviewing the sales numbers could always be replaced with something that will actually affect the sales numbers, such as cleaning your office (more below), which can help with mental clarity and boost your productivity.

Messy Workspace

Allowing your work environment to get disorganized is the last destructive habit to stop. This is where I still struggle the most. I'll get busy. Then things in my car, office, and closet get disorganized, and I start losing things or spending a ton of time finding things. When I do find dead time, I spend it on anything but getting reorganized. There are two things I've found that have helped so far. Again, if you have others email me tyler@thepirateguides.com and let's share them!

The first thing comes from Mr. Shankman himself, and that's to become more minimalistic. Start by taking a few boxes and throwing in them anything you don't see yourself needing today or tomorrow. Tape it up, put it in another room, and, if after six months, you haven't pulled anything from that box, then throw it away or donate it to Goodwill.

The second thing is to reduce decisions. Develop rituals that reduce time spent making decisions on what to wear, where or what to eat, and where to stay. Pick a hotel chain and stick with it. Pick a meal plan and cook all the meals for the week on Sunday. Pick a uniform of sorts and always wear the same combination of things. I'd imagine this last one is easier for a guy, but I'm certain there is a way to minimize wardrobe decisions, at least in some degree, for women as well. The key is to minimize your stuff down to the bare essentials. Like they say in the

Jungle Book, "look for the bare necessities, the simple bare necessities."

Putting It All Together

As with most things in life, change doesn't come easily. However, without self-analysis and continuous improvement, your effectiveness is unlikely to improve.

One of the beautiful things about Peter Shankman's message (and salespeople in general) is that being "different" should be, and usually is, viewed positively.

While most never realize the impact of their bad habits, salespeople have the ability to adapt and change quickly. We are goal-oriented by nature. Present us with a challenge, and we will generally accept it, achieve it, and strive to exceed expectations. Therefore, when it comes to organization, analyze your habits in much the same way someone who has conquered ADHD would, whether you have it or not. Look within yourself for adjustments you can make to improve your health, mindset, and effectiveness. You likely won't need much time to come up with a list. Then grant yourself some dead time, using it to set yourself up to be more productive and to introduce some of your new-found adjustments. Help yourself stay the course with apps and automation tools. Streamline your calendar, contacts, e-mail, etc. by adopting and sticking to one tech ecosystem. Find apps that will remind you and keep you on track. My personal favorite is an app called Productive. It makes habit change easy and fun with reminders, stats, games, and rewards.

Lastly, avoid disruptive and destructive sales behaviors. Having ridden in the field with hundreds of reps, the commonalities here are astounding. Stewing over your sales numbers, good or bad, doesn't change them. It's like watching the clock move or paint dry. It has no impact on the outcome.

Above all else, avoid negative self-talk. When you feel it coming on, remind yourself to turn to a good Ted Talk, podcast, or YouTube video that will inspire and redirect your thoughts. Most importantly, remember we are all in the same boat we just operate it differently. Take control of your emotions and embrace your gifts, ADHD or otherwise!

CHAPTER
Three

YOUR SHIP'S NAME?

The Power of Self Branding

This question of branding was asked of me a couple years ago, and it has stuck with me. Maybe it was because I couldn't answer it on the spot, or maybe it was because I didn't want to be defined by three simple words. Whatever the case, the more I learn about powerful brands, the more important I think this exercise of personal branding is. We all strive to leave our mark, our legacy. Whether it's in business, within our community, our family, our church, or somewhere else we all seek one thing: to be relevant (at least somewhat).

However, let's look at some masterful examples of relevance within each of these categories. In business we might think of Steve Jobs. Community? Possibly MLK. Family? The first name that comes to mind is Danny Tanner (yes, of Full House fame). Church? Joel Osteen popped into my head. What do all these people have in common? You know their brand and could probably describe it for them in three words.

Let's take Joel Osteen, for instance, since Jobs is overdone. I don't even know this guy, nor have I ever seen his sermon, yet I know his brand. He comes across as genuine, honest, and sincere. Because of this, you believe it's about you and not him. This gives you the ability to believe in something bigger than Joel Osteen. If it were about him, even in the slightest, no one would go see him, and the stadiums would be empty.

Or what about TV's most iconic dad, Danny Tanner? Three words: kind, loving, and fun (cheesy). What makes this one so interesting is that if you've ever seen Bob Saget's comedy, you know he's downright raunchy. It almost makes it shocking to see "The Brand" meltdown live before your eyes. And yet every time I see that man, I still think of Danny Tanner. Hell, he played that character so well it ruined his ability to expand his acting roles. Don't believe me? Name another relevant character Bob Saget has played since.

So, from Danny Tanner and Joel Osteen we can learn that we need to define who we are, how we want others to perceive us, and what our "brand" is because it matters. Without it you're just Bob Saget getting roasted at 10 p.m. on Comedy Central by a bunch of washed-up comedians. And that's sad!

Let's break "Naming Your Ship" down into two parts: Self-Analysis and Feedback Analysis. This is a brainstorming activity, and the companion guide at www.thepirateguides.com has a list of additional questions along with a worksheet to help aid you in coming up with your very own personal branding strategy.

STEP 1: Self-Analysis

Brainstorming Your Brand

One of the more insightful exercises I've done in sales training over the years was called the DISC personality and colors assessment test. For those who haven't done this before, it's an exercise in understanding your strengths, weaknesses, personalities, and areas for improvement. If you're trying to formulate key attributes that set you apart from others, this exercise will help.

Personalities are categorized in four colors: Red, Yellow, Green, and Blue. All of us usually have personality traits that show up in each of the four categories, but most people have a dominant color. Red-dominant people tend to be more aggressive, assertive, and goal-oriented. These are the folks who will get a job done, move on to the next thing, and spend little time on minutia. When you think of yellow-dominant people, think of Bart Simpson (also yellow in color). Yellow-dominant personalities like to be the life of the party, make people laugh, win people over with charisma and charm. Like their red counterparts, they tend to spend little time on the details. Blue-personality dominant people are the opposite and therefore are analytical in nature. What reds and yellows lack, blues have in spades. Measurement, statistical analysis, and deep thinking lead their decision making and direction. Green-dominant people match the color and personality of our childhood friend Kermit the Frog. These people are caring, compassionate, empathetic, and the counterpoint to their red counterparts who just want things done!

The companion guide has a link to a free colors personality assessment along with a list of questions to help you formulate your strengths and weaknesses. Ultimately you want to brand yourself in a way that is uniquely value driven and that can be clearly defined. Think in terms of what is needed on your sales team, in your territory, or in your organization, and then tailor specific strengths to fit those needs.

Naming Your Brand

Once you have formulated some idea of what your brand of selling is, go ahead and name it. Why? Because if done correctly it will tell your internal and external customers what your strengths are, which in turn sets expectations.

The Challenger Sales, by Matthew Dixon, popularized not only the four-color wheel, but also branding of a sale's "type." Many companies now know what a challenger salesperson looks like and even seek them out. In a similar way, you can do this on your own sales team and within your own territory. Are you a "trusted advisor," a "challenger," a "collaborator," a "transparent seller," or an "innovator?"

Contrary to what you might guess, based on the title of this book, I did not pick "pirate" as my brand. While I do in fact spend a ton of time learning others' ideas, reading books, and applying knowledge in my own way, "pirate" seemed to work for the book title, but not my sales persona.

Instead I went with "chameleon." When I took the colors assessment, I was the only person they could remember who didn't really fit in a bucket with a dominant category. Much like my chameleon friend, I adapt to the situation and the personality across the table.

Understanding your own personal selling style will help guide you to your own strengths. In addition, this exercise will also, with hope, have you looking at your weaknesses. If you learn to quickly pick up on the color traits of those you are selling to, then you can audible and give the customer only the info he or she wants. Try giving a "red" personality a bunch of data and just watch their head spin. Likewise, try being assertive or demanding in a room that includes even one "green" personality and watch as emails and calls go unreturned after what you thought was a successful sales call.

Tagline Your Brand in Three Words

In the same way you want to name your brand, you also want to find three words that encompass your best attributes. The key is to pick the things that uniquely possess and encompass you, in addition to words others can relate with.

I landed on transparent, fearless, and collaborative. An odd thing happens when you define yourself in these terms. In some cases, you may pick a word that doesn't perfectly describe you, but slowly and surely you embody it because you strive for others to perceive you in that way.

For me this was the case with all three. While I had shown in the personality assessment to carry these traits, I immediately thought of times I wasn't collaborative, fearless, or transparent. Through a focused formulation of these words, I found that I sought to always live by them. I distinctly remember finding myself in a sales calls saying, "am I being transparent enough here?" or "am I avoiding this customer, account, or goal out of fear?" It's a powerful exercise that will not only help define your best attributes for others, but also force you to fully embody them going forward.

STEP 2: Feedback Analysis

Okay, so now that you have a pretty good idea what your brand is through self-analysis, it's time to test it with the take of others and blow the whole thing up! Just kidding. But you will find after some feedback and testing that some things just don't fit or clearly define you.

Email Challenge

This exercise takes a good bit of courage, but I promise it will change your life. Make a list of ten to twenty people you believe know you well professionally and ask them to describe three things they see as your strengths and three areas of weakness. The email can simply say that, "they are among the chosen few whom you respect" and that "you're on a mission for self-improvement. You are writing because "you want to know how others that you trust perceive you both good and bad."

When I did this exercise, I was pretty much spot on with my strengths and downright upset and depressed by my weaknesses. I heard things like "my tone is sometimes too demanding," and "I occasionally interrupt and butt in when others are talking." My dad told me I don't make good eye contact. All these things were of course true and helpful, but it's not always easy to hear hard truths.

One time one of my bosses gave me feedback after a presentation assessment that I used the word "I" 57 times throughout the presentation. My immediate reaction? "Why is she knit-picking and good lord who counts something like this? No way was it actually 57 times!" You know what, though? She was right. The next time I gave a presentation and realized how right she was my stomach sank. However, over time "we" became the pronoun of choice, and slowly but surely my presentations started to feel more inclusive in nature instead of directive.

Test Your Brand Power

Next time you give a presentation or do a performance evaluation, run the branding exercise past some people in person. Look for their reactions and ask questions. Explain to them what you are trying to achieve professionally and look for advice given in return. Remember you want feedback, so make sure you ask open ended questions that elicit a response and challenge people to be honest.

Tweak

No good scientific method is complete without learning from the feedback and using it. You might find you have to redo or rethink your original personal brand, or you may just see that it needs to be more clearly defined. Whatever the case, if you don't need to change something then you probably weren't seeking or listening for feedback.

Embody

Once you have identified and defined your personal brand, add some visualization to make it real. This can be just for you personally or it could be something you share with your sales team if you'd like them to understand your key attributes better. Don't go adding it to your business card, LinkedIn profile, or email signature, though—this is for you alone. However, you should put it in places you can see it as a reminder to embody this new brand identity. Once ingrained, your subconscious will take over, and you will start to see that you deliver more value both with your internal and external customers.

Putting It All Together

Want to improve your sales game and career trajectory while avoiding the pitfalls and pigeonholes that plagued Bob Saget? One of the simplest ways of doing so is to develop and uniquely position your brand. When you spend time understanding not only the strengths you have now, but also the strengths you need to develop, you in turn create core principles that will guide you to success. What has worked for the biggest TV personalities and consumer brands can work for you. Start with a goal of describing yourself in three words. Then analyze through feedback, along with trial and error, looking for response. Once you have identified the qualities and strengths that seemingly resonate with your core tribe, develop and center your actions around them. Be the brand and embody the characteristics that draw a connection with people. Name your ship!

CHAPTER
Four

YOUR DESTINATION AND WAYPOINTS

Goal Setting – Stretch Goals and S.M.A.R.T Goals

Growing up in poverty, in the hands of abusive parents and a pimp for a father, David's view of himself was based solely on how others saw him. He was a pudgy kid with low self-esteem and was bullied relentlessly. Over time he grew to hate himself as his family skipped towns trying to escape the problems that seemed to follow them everywhere. At 16, he dropped out of school. At 18, he joined the Army, seeing it as the only honorable path to fixing himself. Like so many other things in life, this too would prove to be a short-lived home for David. After boot camp and several months of training he was diagnosed with sickle cell and forced to quit.

28

For David, the choice seemed out of his control. Everything and everyone appeared to be against him. For the next several years, he continued to move around, picking up one terrible job after another. By the time he was 24 years old, David found himself 175 pounds overweight, severely depressed, and filled with despair.

That was until he saw a documentary on Navy Seals that moved him to take ownership of his path. It was then that he made a seemingly impossible stretch goal of joining the SEALS. The plan would be to get in shape and force his way onto the SEAL team.

But, as motivated and determined as David was in that moment, he still had a major problem. He weighed nearly 300 pounds, and no recruiter on earth was going to let him in the Army, much less let him go through SEAL training. In addition, not only was he not in shape, but he also had the issue of sickle cell trait to deal with.

This time something was different, though. David didn't seem to think in terms of obstacles. He knew he had to change his life and thus decided to break down his goal into achievable, measurable, and specific chunks. His first day working out, he barely managed to run a quarter mile. The next day his body hurt so badly he had to walk the same quarter mile. But he kept pushing, kept moving, and continued setting new goals. Slowly but surely, he started hitting longer distances and losing more weight. He ate right, worked hard, praised himself for hitting new milestones, and kept trudging on.

With three months left to go until SEAL camp, David found himself still needing to lose about 103 pounds. At this point, most people would have given up, but not David. He showed up at SEAL camp slightly overweight, but still in the best shape of his life. Over the course of that year, David ended up having to repeat "hell week" not once, but twice! However, he achieved what he set out for. He became a Navy SEAL and to this day remains the only person to have gone through "hell week" three times!

Today, David Goggin's holds about 60 other records for endurance training and ultra-marathons. He is a motivational speaker, best-selling author, and most importantly he is happy. When asked on a Joe Rogan Podcast, what the turning point was, he said, "You gotta face your fears, man up, and set goals for yourself. I had to invent a guy that didn't exist. I had to invent a guy that could take any pain, any suffering, and any judgement. I started using 'what if' in a positive line of questioning only and pictured myself achieving. It just became a different mindset. I turned negatives into positives and persisted at all costs."

STEP 1: PICK YOUR DESTINATION

Stretch Goals

Setting stretch goals can be tricky. You don't want to set a goal that's unachievable, but you also don't want to sell yourself short. Think in a similar way to David. When trying to pick your destination, ask yourself, is this something above all else that I want to achieve? Then ask yourself if it's within reason to think you could attain it. Finally, and most importantly, ask yourself this ever-important question, "Can I *commit* to achieving this?" Commitments are different than other loosely defined goals. Marriage is a commitment. Running a marathon is a commitment. Winning the lottery is not. When you can answer yes to all three of these questions, you have found your stretch goal.

In the companion PDF at the end of the book you will find three brainstorm sets that will help you formulate the goal and set the vision. You can find questions and worksheets to aid in the process along with other tips and tricks at in the back of the book or by downloading the PDF from www.thepirateguides.com.

Challenge Your Perception

Often in sales when we are trying to set goals for ourselves, we set them off benchmarks. However, within your own company or sales teams it's very likely that groupthink has set in. Groupthink is a psychological phenomenon where, over time, members of a group begin to lose creativity, or fear stretching their boundaries, because of past experiences. When you're challenging your perception you likely will need to go outside of the benchmarks and preconceived notions held by your own team or even company. Whenever possible, look for examples of what is being achieved elsewhere in your industry or by other top performers. Then, in true pirate fashion, call these people up and ask them as many questions as you can. Often you will find that what they are doing is replicable and possibly even reasonable. Finally, apply your findings to your own territory, sales unit, or business.

Cast a Vision

After pirating some good intel and comparing it to what you have in front of you, it's time to cast a vision. What is the time commitment you will need? What might you need to change? What is the path going to look like to get to your destination? What roadblocks and snags might you anticipate? Visualization is one of the strongest attributes behind most successes. As they say, "seeing is believing."

Make Your Destination Visible

Now that you have your vision it helps to go a step further and make it visible. By doing this you will add a certain ownership to your goal. If it's an individual goal, then this might be as simple as posting the goal somewhere where you, and even others, will see it. If you are a manager or business owner, however, your destination visualization might need to be a little more creative and enlightening.

Though some call him crazy, Elon Musk is famous for this. When Elon opened his then very young company, SpaceX, he posted a giant mural of Mars draped with skyscrapers, human inhabitants, and flying (Tesla?) cars. Whether or not this was an achievable stretch goal, or a dream, didn't matter. The picture inspired the employees to believe they were working together on something profound and life changing. It gave everyone a sense that their work was bigger than what could be achieved as individuals, and it cast a vision of where they were heading.

Like David's Navy SEAL vision or Elon's Mars vision, set your goals high and really visualize yourself getting there. By doing so you will have all the fuel needed to persevere above and beyond the obstacles and snags.

STEP 2: SET YOUR WAYPOINTS

S.M.A.R.T. Goals: Your Controllable(s)

When setting S.M.A.R.T. goals, we also need to follow a method similar to David's. Stretch your vision of what is possible and then apply shorter, more attainable and measurable benchmarks that plot the path.

Many today use the S.M.A.R.T. goal method when setting such benchmarks. Originally documented by George T. Doran in 1981, the acronym S.M.A.R.T. stands for: specific, measurable, assignable, realistic, and time bound. Many have written about it since, including the bestselling author Charles Duhigg. Charles goes so far as to explain that in writing his new book, *Smarter, Faster, Better,* that he was "stuck" and "couldn't seem to appropriate his time to write a book, prepare for an upcoming TV show, and complete his required commitments." Ironically, the book he was writing was on the best practices of people who achieve and seemingly never run out of time. Yet, Charles himself couldn't seem to find the time. It wasn't until a colleague pointed out that he wasn't applying his own learnings that he "woke up."

As Charles explains it, "I needed to have a system that gave me more constraints and boundaries." So, what did he do? He started tackling his days in specific, measurable, assignable, realistic, and time bound ways. He would set a goal for when and what he would get done, put parameters on how it could be done, and limit daily and even hourly interruption unless it fit his predetermined plan. By doing this it gave him control to assign or decline and put him in the driver's seat of his own progress.

Specific

Formulate a list of specific things that need to be done over the next 30, 60, and 90 days. Start to outline what benchmarks you would like to see hit, along with an understanding of obstacles that might inhibit your achievable(s). Much like your stretch goals, begin to prioritize the list based on the three questions. Can this be achieved? Does this need to be achieved above other things? And, finally, can I commit to achieving it? Once you have done this exercise, you should be able to whittle down your list to the few most important goals and eliminate those that aren't essential.

Measurable

As Peter Drucker famously once said, "if you can't measure it, you can't improve it." There is a reason people often fail to meet their goals, and often times it has nothing to do with skill, but instead, a lack of proper measurement.

Let's use the local gym as an example. If you visit your local gym on January 1, you'll notice the parking lot is fuller, the machines are all taken, and the faces look far less familiar. Oddly, though, by February 1 things seem to be back to normal. Why is that? Are we all inherently lazy?

Studies show that people are far more likely to achieve success with a personal trainer. While there are a multitude of reasons for this, one of them has to do with accountability and measurement. With little expertise and no accountability, people with the best intentions of sticking to a new workout often give up if they don't achieve weight loss fast enough. However, is it possible they were achieving desirable results and weren't measuring the right things? What if someone took measurements on January 1 for body fat percentage, cholesterol levels, and hormone levels, in addition to weight? Might that person have shed body fat but picked up muscle weight and improved on every other statistic? Or what about diet? Did the person destroy the improvements they might have seen from the gym by increasing consumption of the wrong types of food? One thing is for certain: if you only measure success with one variable, or on the wrong set of variables, you will only have anecdotal evidence to support you.

Assignable

Now that you have the goals you're targeting and how you're going to measure them, it's time to understand an ownership plan. What parts of this venture can you increase results on through calling on your fellow shipmates? And, furthermore, what things must you captain yourself?

In medical sales, people often have a breadth of under-utilized inside salespeople, clinical resources, top customers (KOLs—KEY OPINION LEADERS), etc. While things can often be done by a lone wolf, most can be done more easily or efficiently when you implore your ground troops. Every company has a set of resources that can help in one manner or another. By understanding up front how you can utilize these to the best of your abilities, you'll in turn free yourself up for the key items that you yourself will captain. In some instances, this might be as simple as asking a sales manager, or sales ops, to produce the desired measurements so that you can track it without it falling on your own reconnaissance.

Realistic

Obviously unrealistic goals aren't helpful, and many of us don't set out to have them be as such. The real value is in understanding where the obstacles might derail your best intentions. Here is where you can set parameters to allow when and where there should be wiggle room. In some instances, you might miss a 30-day mark, but know with full confidence you will make it up and still hit the 90-day mark. In other instances, like the gym, you may be able to say the sales are coming because of other measurements pointing to future weight loss. Use realistic optimism, not self-defeating reflection.

Time Bound

Try to avoid setting S.M.A.R.T goals that can't be parametrized by time. The challenge is that salespeople in particular need a deadline. Without one, we often wait until the last minute or push things to the next day. Let's face it, ADHD might get over-diagnosed, but we all have a bit of it in us. Set time constraints for your work. Hold yourself accountable or have someone else hold you accountable. Include time in your work for things that improve your mood, health, or well-being. Your plan needs to include a certain element of sustainability, or else you might fall short at the finish line.

One of the ways I do this is by using calendar reminders linked to a task list. Years ago, when I realized I had procrastination issues, I found that if I broke a goal up into individual benchmarks, with time constraints, I could in fact work ahead. However, as someone who needs a reminder to do almost anything, the more I broke down goals into smaller chunks, the longer my to-do list got. To solve this, I ended up tying my task list to calendar notifications. This way I'm constantly reminded of my own destination procrastination. Until I complete a desired task, I continue to get more and more calendar notifications. As a response, panic and a sense of urgency starts to kick in and push me to focus. It's akin to those who always run late and change their clocks in an effort to trick their brain. It works, and you can do it with every goal or task.

Putting It All Together

Let's use this book for example. Each week I will set goals for myself on what chapter composition, editing, or marketing endeavor I plan to achieve. I add the specific tasks to my reminder list and put dates and times in for completion. This week's list included preparing for an interview and discussion with Peter Shankman mentioned in the last chapter, writing and completing S.M.A.R.T goals, researching topics and stories for closing strategies (which we will cover later), and working on the website design. As I complete each task, I check the box and avoid notifications. If I fall behind, I'm hit with several daily notifications that trigger slight panic. Urgency then sets in and I adjust accordingly. Try a similar method with an upcoming long-term goal. Break down the goal into short and attainable benchmarks and come up with a strategy to create urgency and accountability. Goal setting is nothing new to those of us in sales, but getting the most out of your goals can always be improved. Practice the skill, and once you master it, you'll become almost superhuman in productivity.

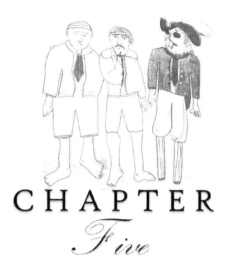

CHAPTER
Five

CAPTAIN AND CREW

Influence and Human Behavior

Learn to captain your own ship and treat your crew like you'd want to be treated. Chapter five is all about learning to be a captain through influence and an understanding of human behavior. If you are thinking, "how does this apply to me? I don't want to be a leader, nor do I want to influence my peers," then feel free to skip this chapter. However, before doing so, keep in mind that our success, whether we admit it or not, often depends on the actions and thoughts of others. Imagine the early explorers setting sail by themselves on solo missions. As much as I admire Amelia Earhart's spirit and the legacy that led to iconic representation for the women's movement, her solo journey, after all, was a failed mission. While there is no shortage of exemplary solo results and resolve through history, most great journeys are done with the aid of others. As Helen Keller put it, "Alone we can do so little; together we can do so much."

From an evolutionary standpoint, humans were built to achieve results with very little. It was coded deep within our DNA to create from the world around us. It should come as no surprise then that taking a trip back to our roots might provide a lot of insight on how to succeed in the present, right? However, we live in a world where a decision on what color to use in a new toilet paper ad can lead to debate and internal corporate turmoil, and where even being the VP of TP can at times feel like anything but(t) (pardon the pun) an executive level job. What if such failings and petty squabbles were a result of a penchant for short-sightedness that could be cured by that act of reflecting on the past and considering inherent human behavioral patterns?

Some of the best sales leaders have taken to heart that simplicity and humility go further than hierarchy and management. In a sense, understanding human behavior and influence hasn't changed, but our environment has. Some of the most brilliant minds and leaders in this world take a "leaders' eat last approach" and aim to influence instead of instructing. Let's first look at such an idea and analyze some similarly altruistic and progressive concept. With any luck, having a better understanding of our species will change how we approach selling to them, and with them.

Step 1: Seek to Understand

Letting Your Crew Eat First – Pirated Tips

Here's a rundown of several challenges relating to human behavior, history, and individual personality that you'll surely face on your journey. I've tagged a book to read for each issue and expanded a bit on those texts. With a little bit of work, it's possible to build a library geared towards more effectively understanding and working alongside your fellow humans, whether in sales or elsewhere in life.

Understanding Your Fellow Shipmates Better

Turn to *The Lessons of History* for help. Written by Will and Ariel Durant in 1968, this book is a summary of an eleven-volume lifelong dedication to history called *The Story of Civilization*. These two Pulitzer Prize winning authors started this mission on the premise that history, studied the normal way, is flawed. As such, it's often presented as just a snapshot in time, written from the perspectives of a few, and then "updated" over and over. Like the telephone game of old, every update and translation creates more inaccuracies. So how did two people avoid then doing the same thing? Simple, they read thousands and thousands of years of documents looking only for consistencies. Their resulting conclusions shed light on something interesting. Every culture and every civilization faced many of the same problems we still face today: racism, religious strife, government issues, war, growth and decay, progress and regress, just to name a few. What's the takeaway here then? Well, while civilization and technology might change, human nature apparently does not. Understanding why we do what we do is the most important step in progress.

Go Beyond the Shallow Depths of Personality

For help here, pick up *Principles: Life and Work*, by Ray Dalio, who has been called the Steve Jobs of the financial industry and rightfully so. He changed the way we invest, how we invest, wrote many of the early computer algorithms on picking what we invest in, and was even instrumental in McDonald's launching the Chicken McNugget! However, it's Dalio's approach to human behavior that many large companies have adopted and studied. His company, Bridgewater, had all their employees do a deep dive and publish their own core principles. Then they created baseball cards for each other with their stats on the back. Knowing your own and each other's strengths, weaknesses, personality traits, principles and core values, and, being reminded of them routinely, creates a mutual respect that becomes the foundation for growth.

Define Your Mission and Course

*The Subtle Art of Not Giving a F*ck: A Counterintuitive Approach to Living A Good Life,* by Mark Manson can provide an assist on this one.

While Manson is no Will or Ariel Durant, he's experienced life in such a way that he has arrived at many of the same conclusions that even Dalio found so helpful. In a life full of distractions, a focus on finding your purpose and defining your core principles will create transformation. It's a simple premise, but hard to enact. However, success can and will only happen once it's done.

We all know you can't have too many goals or be great at too many things. We also know that it takes focus to achieve your dreams. However, how many of us chase surface or false goals of promotion, increased pay, a bigger this or a better that, without ever feeling happy? This is because even if you achieve that surface goal, if it wasn't a goal driven by your purpose or mission, then you find yourself holding up a plastic trophy, which, once in hand, doesn't feel that spectacular.

Let Your Crew Do Some of the Sailing

Doing it all is a failing endeavor. So, learn to build your network, and let others help you along the way by reading *How to Win Friends and Influence People* by Dale Carnegie. While the book was written in 1936, its lessons still apply today.

No one wins an argument and self-promotion is the entryway to the law of diminishing returns. We all find ourselves in arguments from time to time and if you are like me, it's hard not to want to see your point across and win. The challenge is, even if you can win, you end up making the other person feel defeated, silly, and worst yet hating you. We can all probably think of times when we lost an argument, did actually learn something from it, but vowed to avoid doing that with that person ever again. Carnegie's book teaches empathy, understanding, putting others first, and letting others win from time to time. Think of the parent that lets the kid win to build their confidence. The result isn't embarrassing because it wasn't about winning it was about future progress.

Understand Your Shipmates One Thing

Real behavioral change doesn't happen without understanding human behavior first. To help learn that hard lesson, turn to *The Power of Habit* Written by Charles Duhigg.

Think of it this way: if Will and Ariel Durant studied 5,000 years of history only to find that human nature hasn't changed since the caveperson, then we aren't going to be able to change each other without starting from a level of understanding. We are hard-wired to do everything a certain way. If you want to see a change in culture, attitude, health and appearance, drive, or motivation, then start with focusing on changing *one* thing.

Duhigg dedicates a chapter in his book to cultural change as it relates to large corporations. He documents the work of Paul O'Neill as CEO of Alcoa. Paul was brought into Alcoa as the new CEO from outside the company in 1987. He was immediately met with resistance by almost everyone for a laser focus stance on worker safety. It was all he ever talked about during a time when the company needed to show a return to its shareholders. However, O'Neill's logic had less to do with worker safety and more to do with his understanding of human nature. Not one worker in the company could argue or deny the importance of worker safety in factories with large industrial equipment that could dismember or even kill a man. Safety was a unified rally cry that everyone could get behind and stand for. The results led to many other incremental changes under O'Neill's leadership, and the company grew from 3 billion to 27.5 billion in revenues.

STEP 2: Influence Over Enforcement

Pirated Tips: Reciprocity, Scarcity, and Consensus

One of the leading minds on influence is Dr. Robert Cialdini. As a psychologist, author, speaker, and professor, much of his career and life has centered on learning the art of persuasion. In his best-selling book, *Influence: The Psychology of Persuasion,* Dr. Cialdini goes through six proven and scientifically backed principles that have been shown to increase the chances of someone saying yes. We will review three of them here, in relation to selling, and will specifically go through examples of use in medical sales.

Reciprocity

Reciprocity quite possibly could be the strongest influencer, and there's a right and a wrong way to use it. Ever have someone offer you a free gift only to then turn around and ask for your wallet or checkbook to make a donation? They were trying to use the law of reciprocity. Studies have shown that we feel an obligation to return favors. The problem, as with most things that work, is that the use of reciprocity is overused and often disingenuous. In order to make the law of reciprocity work when influencing others, you have to offer something of real value. Furthermore, your intent should be genuine. When done correctly, this tactic can have tremendous influence.

Let's roll through examples in medical sales (though the application could be implored in nearly any industry). Let's say you're trying to get a doctor to trial your new device, drug, test, or equipment. Years ago, you could have given some product away for free. That, however, would be disingenuous in today's world. This rule of reciprocity, when used in this way, was so strong that it led to strict laws prohibiting the giving away of any item of value. No longer can you give away product of any kind to a doctor and for good reason. If you think about it, you don't want the doctors treating you or your loved ones with products just because the company had deep pockets and could afford to take huge losses to recoup future gains.

This being said, you can still achieve reciprocity in many other ways. What else could you give to your doctor or hospital of value that would result in them wanting to in turn help you? Maybe it's your time, your expertise, or simply a commitment to being there and lending support at all hours of the day.

I've found that the easiest way to help a doctor, in particular, is with his or her business. Doctors will tell you they feel cheated having not gotten good business educations as part of their curriculum. Therefore, if you're savvy in this area, you have a lot to offer. Try to think outside the box and ask a lot of questions. Learn about your physician's business or gain understanding on how they are paid. Can you improve efficiency? Can you increase profit margin? Can you decrease readmissions or improve outcomes? What can you or your product offer of value that can be measured and reported back? Once you identify this and prove you can generate results, you will quickly see a shift in your favor.

Years ago, I used to sell surgical equipment for gynecology. At the time a number of doctors were in private practice and split time between the hospital and their office. If possible, they preferred to stay in the office where reimbursement and margins were higher, but without access to equipment and anesthesia, they were forced to do procedures in the hospital. That was until we fixed that problem by helping them set up in-office procedures by linking them to mobile anesthesia companies who would bill insurance directly at a fraction of the cost. The anesthesia companies saw greater margins at this site of service, too, and thus were also all about it. Often times they would bring all the equipment needed and bill insurance for it separately. Patients benefited because they saw the office setting as more laid back and comfortable. In addition, the lower overhead costs at the doctor's office lead to lower patient bills. Thus, for a short period of time we found a win-win-win scenario, and the results proved it.

Over the course of a couple years, any doctor you could move fully to the office, would double, if not triple, his or her volume. Why? Well, if more patients can afford it, and the doctors and anesthesiologists can make more money, then you are going to see an uptick in volume. Opportunities like this exist and don't last that long, so you must evaluate the market and jump on them. By being the first to offer something new and of value, you can reap huge benefits.

Scarcity

The second proven influence on human behavior is scarcity. In economies of scale the more something increases in demand and decreases in volume the higher its price. The same thing goes for the scales of the human mind. If you can be one of the few, or the first or last person with something, then you're viewed in higher status.

Let's say you're launching a new product. Where do you go and who do you approach first with your new test, drug, or device? Look no further than to the doctors or hospitals that are progressive. More often than not this information can be found through asking around or in simple Google searches. As a rule of thumb, early adopters are habitual and remain early adopters for everything. Find them, bring them value, build up their ego and prowess, and watch as they sell for you.

Consensus

Now we reach consensus, the last of Dr. Cialdini three tactics for influence that we'll discuss. Call it social norms or call it strength in numbers, but one thing is for sure: if others are doing it, you have a better chance of it spreading. Look at the number of advertisements that use customer or patient reviews backed in large-numbers studies to prove something works. When something new lacks hard evidence of its actual success, we look to other human beings around us to verify efficacy through their personal experiences with a product or service.

Where scarcity works for early adopters, consensus works for the rest of us. Use your early adopters to build out case studies and data that can be shared. Any time you can walk into a doctor's office or hospital with a list of other reputable users, your chances of trial adoption skyrocket. Consensus is both the proof that others see value in what you have and the evidence supporting the claim it's achieved success elsewhere already.

Pick your early adopters wisely and choose doctors or health systems in good standing in the community. Start small and in places that can act fast and do everything in your power to make sure it goes well. Track and metric the outcomes and data, and then ask if you can share it. It's the reason KOLs exist and are still used so often. Without the support of peers, you will struggle mightily to get a foothold into any new territory or customer segment.

Putting It All Together

So, what can we learn from these lessons on human behavior and influence? In short, human nature has changed very little and age-old principles of influence still work.

The environment is all that really changes, and it does so today faster and with more regularity than it ever has before. Be creative in your solutions and strategic in your approach. Find areas to add value, pick good early adopters, and start small. By starting small you can move more quickly and test theories and hypothesis more rapidly.

Once something seems to be working, then make sure you set up a system to track and measure it so the data can later be shared. Spread your message and value proposition from the inside out and be consistent. If you have one doc using something in a large group or system, then hit the rest of the docs and system next. Build a reputation of being a trusted advisor and avoid anything and everything that could reduce your credibility. If you can do all this correctly, you will see results.

CHAPTER
Six

THE ANCHOR

Anchor the Sale in the Why

Now that we've learned a little about the voyage we are going to take, picked our destination, named the ship, and assembled the captain and crew, it's time to pull the anchor. Rest assured, you won't get very far in today's selling environment without pulling the anchor and finding "the why" buried deep below your vessel.

This is a crucial step, so, if it's ok with you, we're going to slow down and take our time here. But worry not, our time will be spent in helpful stories. You'll hear from the "Iceman" Wim Hof and from the "Whyman" Simon Sinek, and then we'll frame up the applications in some real-world examples. So, let's pull the anchor and get started.

The Iceman Cometh

It was a cold Sunday morning in Sittard, Netherlands, when a then young man named, Wim Hof, felt a sudden urge to plunge himself through a

44

thin sheet of ice covering the Beatrixpark canal and into the subfreezing waters below. Moments later, and much to his surprise, he felt a deep calm and clarity as he exited the water. As Hof explained on a podcast with Joe Rogan, "I, like many, was on something of a soul search and I found the cold to have my answers."

Hof had previously read hundreds of books on eastern philosophy, yoga, meditation, and the like, yet he could never find what he was looking for. Having lost his wife, whom had suffered from mental illness, to suicide, Hof found himself depressed and in charge of caring for his four young children. "I couldn't think, I just had to be," explained Hof. The kids needed him, and he needed to find peace within himself. No one could bring his beautiful wife back, and no one could fix the pain he felt. If he was going to prevail and be the father his kids needed, he would have to do it himself. For Hof this reason and clarity came to him in the cold icy waters of the Beatrixpark canal.

Today Wim, now called the "Iceman" by many, holds some 30 Guinness book of world records for some of the most inconceivable feats of human endurance. He's climbed Everest and Mt. Kilimanjaro in shorts, submerged himself in subzero water for hours on end with no drop-in body temperature, and he hold records for marathons in both the hottest and coldest climates on earth. In recent years, he has started garnering more world fame as he has taught others his methods and allowed the scientific community to test him. His methods are now practiced by millions, including myself, and are both simple and life changing.

If you were to ask Hof his "why," he would tell you that everyone deserves the right to be "happy, healthy, and strong." Having experienced the sudden and traumatic death of his wife, he realized that life for him and his kids would be nothing without finding answers. The answers came from within, brought on by a calling to cold water, and his life's purpose became helping others not only endure, but survive in happiness.

Using Wim as an example then, let's pretend we didn't know his why or story. It took him 15 years to start getting his word and method out to the masses, and he's still a relative unknown in comparison to other celebrity types with much less to offer. There have been hundreds of "methods" and "gurus" who have been debunked and come and gone. In fact, New York Times author Scott Carney set out to write his now top-selling book, *What Doesn't Kill Us,* to do just that. Having debunked other famous cult leaders and gurus, Scott booked a plane ticket to the Netherlands intent on finding flaw and phony. What he found instead in Hof was something he almost couldn't comprehend. The methods worked, and they worked fast! Not only was Wim not a phony, but he was teaching countless others his method for free. Scott himself couldn't believe the changes his mind, body, and spirit were making in such a short span of time. As he entrenched himself in Wim's methods and questioned every oddity, Scott went from sceptic to full-blown believer. The book he originally thought would debunk Wim, instead became an all-out embrace.

Having read Scott's book, done Wim's method, and watched tons of interviews with him, I'm a firm believer that it was Wim's "why" that both delayed his exposure and has since propelled his fame. On the surface, when you hear about a guy climbing Everest in shorts and no shirt and subjecting himself to every harsh environment on earth, you think he's simply crazy. It's not until you understand where this started and what his purpose is that you begin to understand who he is and what he's really about. Without the "why," Wim looks like he's exploiting himself for fame, fortune, or some other unknown cause with bad intention. Once you understand what he personally overcame, that he lives very modestly, and that he's reinvested the earnings thus far into research and training programs for others, you begin to take a deeper look. Thus, in a sense he himself is nothing without the "why."

So, then, how do we uncover the "why" sooner, and what do we do with it once we do? We will address two different methods that very much encompass the "why" philosophy in business and in sales, looking first at Simon Sinek and his messaging, and then at the Lean/Six Sigma methodology.

Simon Sinek Method

In 2010, Simon Sinek gave a Ted Talk entitled *How Great Leaders Inspire Action.* In it he describes what he calls, "The Golden Circle." The golden circle is made up of three rings: what, how, and why. As Sinek explains it, most organizations and salespeople start with what they do, how they do it, or how it works, rarely, if ever, touching on *why* they exist. The "why," as he explains it, "is not for profit or money, that's an outcome, but instead it's a purpose."

He uses the example of computers. Many computer companies will explain that they have the smartest, fastest, thinnest devices, and that they will make your life or organization run more efficiently. Apple, however, uses a different tact. They reverse the order of the what-how-why continuum, starting instead with the why, and it sounds much more inspiring. At Apple, they "think differently" and want to challenge the status quo and change the world. They do so through hiring the most brilliant minds in the world and immersing them in this culture of innovation. And "oh yeah, they also make computers."

"That," says Simon, "is how you sell the why!"

Start with the Why

The point then that Simon makes in this famous Ted Talk that has now been viewed more than 100 million times is that we are nothing without an understanding of our purpose and the why of our customers. How often do we start with what we sell or have, follow with how it works, and never look at what actually inspires the customer to take action?

Let's use an example in the medical industry. Say you have a device or drug that will improve the outcomes of patients. Does the doctor you're selling it to believe their patients have a real problem with this issue? Do they even care? Are they driven by liability, money, or patient care? Do they prefer consultative work or surgery? Do they see themselves in competition with their partners or other doctors in the community, and if so, how do they differentiate themselves? Why did they become a doctor and are they still a doctor for the same reason? Often, we have no answers to these questions prior to selling whatever device or drug we have. We make assumptions perhaps, but are they even correct? Many of the answers to these questions would undoubtedly change your sales approach and speed up the sales cycle. Spend a little time uncovering the answers and you will find your message and conversations vastly improve.

Lean/Six Sigma Method

From a practical approach, uncovering the why might be a little more challenging than just asking a few questions. If you want to get this right and speed up your sales cycle, then the best method for doing so might come from the Lean/Six Sigma method popularized by Japanese car manufacturer Toyota. Lean thinking, in a sense, was years ahead of Simon in its approach to the why. While American car manufacturers were mass producing, the Japanese were paying attention to the customer needs both internally and externally. It realized that quality and customization could be achieved with efficiency. Today its methods are applied in almost every industry and are taught in companies and universities all over the world. Lean thinking is complex and detail-oriented, so we aren't going to cover it soups to nuts here, but we will touch on three concepts that should help in uncovering the why: Go to the Gemba, Five Why Analysis, and Root Cause Theory.

Go to the Gemba

Gemba is a Japanese term meaning "the actual place." In lean thinking you will often hear the term "go to the gemba" in reference to going to the actual physical place of work to see with your own eyes how things are done. The reason: at times it's impossible for us to completely get the picture of what a customer is dealing with without seeing it with our own eyes.

There's an old story, likely part true and part parable, that highlights this very thing.

A toothpaste factory has a problem. It's getting complaints from its distributor that stores and customers are getting toothpaste boxes packaged with empty tubes inside. People are supposed to check the boxes on assembly, but once the boxes are sealed, it's hard to tell with the naked eye whether each box is heavy and thus full. So, the company sends out a task force of engineers to devise a plan. What the engineers come up with is a weighted scale system placed at a point in assembly where it can alarm, and alert should there be a disparity. It would cost only five million dollars and take 12 weeks for the install and training of employees. The plan would put them under budget and on time.

After reviewing the plan, the task force is given the green light to go ahead with implementation. The first two weeks of results show marked improvement in fixing the problem of empty boxes. However, after just a few days, a new problem starts to surface. The alarm that had been set up to alert the floor was being turned off. One of the engineers decided to go back to the floor to see (the gemba) and to understand what was going on. What he found surprised and befuddled them all. The floor manager had explained that the alarm kept sounding and therefore they decided to place a box fan on a table ahead of the scale to blow the boxes off the line to avoid the seemingly continuous sirens. Understanding this wasn't the intended use of the new high-tech solution but seeing that it in fact worked better and would be even cheaper over time, the team decided to implement the box fan solution everywhere.

Now, had that task force spent more time on the floor, or had it gone to the gemba faster, it would have saved five million dollars and 12 weeks' time. But that's not even the biggest problem here. What was the opportunity cost above and beyond the five million dollars in training employees that in fact had the answer to the problem the whole time? Surely none of them needed training on how to use a box fan. The truth of this story is that there are so many simple, effective, and inexpensive solutions that come from those closest to the problem. Find those people to find your answers.

Five Why Analysis

A full understanding of the problem and root cause is imperative to solution selling. For example, in the toothpaste box example, was the root cause unawareness on the part of the workers? Was it a training issue? Was there too much opportunity in the process for human error? Imagine how much time, energy, and money could have been saved by the toothpaste factory had it started with the box fan solution first.

The purpose of five why analysis is to undercover these problems early and to find the root causes of issues. It's a simple task that entails, just as the name suggests, asking "why" five different times and ways. While this might seem simple, think how many times we fail to ask why even once? Most salespeople I've encountered, myself included, work fast and are "fixers" by nature. We think we see a problem. We think we understand it and what is causing it. Then we offer a solution. Sometimes our solution works. Often, we learn how to sell to certain customer types we've seen before. Let me ask you a question, though. Have you ever really looked at your book of business closely and realized all your biggest wins and customers look alike? The reason for this is that as we become experienced and start having success, we tend to be able to shorten the sales cycle in the customer segments where we understand their problems and business pretty well. However, all of us have huge pools of potential customers that we rarely get any business from, and that's often because we don't actually *understand* their business, even though we think we know.

Let's look at an example. I'm in the business of selling genetic testing for hereditary cancer. Of all cancer, only about 15 percent is currently thought to be caused by a hereditary syndrome. When a person has concerning personal and family history risk factors that could be indicative of one of these syndromes, they can have a panel test to evaluate the common associated genes. Often these panels will evaluate 25 to 50 genes that are associated with eight or so types of cancers. These commonly include genes associated with breast, ovarian, colorectal, endometrial, prostate, pancreatic, and gastric cancers.

Having previously worked in women's health selling surgical equipment and screening diagnostics to OB/GYNS, I did what most would have done and started selling these panels to my old customers. I understood these customers' workflow, their challenges, and the complexities they encountered having two specialties pulling at their time. My assumption was that selling them on the concept of screening their patients for hereditary cancer would be easy with my prior knowledge.

However, six months into the job, I realized my best relationships and prior knowledge were getting me no traction. What I soon came to realize was that what made a good customer in my previous job, in the exact same specialty, did not make a great customer in my new one. So, I started reaching out to OBGYNS who I hadn't previously worked with and asking questions. I used the knowledge I had of the specialty to ask good, open-ended questions and started uncovering the problem.

What I found was that I was seemingly up against a challenge that I soon made analogous to recycling. You see, every doctor would tell me they believed in hereditary cancer screening, and most even said they routinely tested. But, behind the scenes, only about 7 to 10 percent of appropriate patients were being worked up. Much like recycling, they couldn't see or fully understand the impact, and, most importantly, they didn't have a good system. Asking why questions then allowed me to uncover the problems, draw parallels, and start working up solutions. It was an exercise done out of necessity, but by the end of my first year I'd seemingly uncovered something most other seasoned sales reps hadn't. I quickly went from running a territory that was a bottom feeder to leading the stack racks of nearly 200 other talented salespeople.

Root Cause Theory

Every product, invention, and good idea solves some sort of problem. Understanding what that problem, is and why someone would buy, requires finding that anchor and pulling that to the surface. Nearly every training, sales book, and seminar, centers around the actual sales pitch. However, like the scenario I encountered when starting in hereditary cancer sales, your pitch is only as good as the problem it solves. My pitch those first six months was finely honed, practiced, and poignant, but it didn't address the underlying root cause of the problem. At its very core, root cause theory is the why behind the buy. Getting to that why requires analyzing the current state and casting a vision for what the future state will look like.

Current State

Think of addressing a customer's needs as a scientific method. The goal is to use why analysis to uncover a problem. Once identified, take action to address the problem on a small scale. In a sense you want to test your hypothesis here but operate under an assumption that you still don't know the answers. With your test in place, set up a system of metrics to check and balance the results. Then analyze, tweak, and adjust.

In lean thinking, they refer to this process as PDCA (Plan, Do, Check, Adjust). Tech startups are the masters of this. It's where the term "fail fast" comes from. The goal is to hypothesize, test, check, and adjust without making too many assumptions and wasting time. The less you can operate on assumption in the current state, and the more you objectively address problems, the better your solutions will be to any customer's needs.

In order to most effectively analyze the current state, go to the gemba. Ask a lot of why questions, take notes, and start hypothesizing problems. Force yourself to see the customer's business through his or her eyes and immerse yourself in what he or she is feeling. Then take your notes, do a simple workup of what you uncovered, and share it with the customer. Ask more questions, and, if necessary, revisit areas that still seem unclear.

Future State

Once you have analyzed the current state and have shared your findings with the customer, it's time to cast a vision. Work up a value proposition centered on his or her needs. Tell them what you plan to do for them based on your findings and ask them how you can prove and track the results. Define success with numbers and metrics that can be tracked. Is the goal to reduce costs, improve efficiency, or change outcomes? Or is it to drive customer revenue, improve margins, or differentiate from competition? How can you track this to prove the solutions are working?

In medical sales this can be helpful because doctors are often too busy to analyze their own business. Remember how many will tell you they felt cheated having not gotten any business school, only to later find themselves running a business? This is where you can be of the most value. By understanding your customers' business and finding areas where you can provide value, you'll prove your worth no matter the industry.

Putting It All Together

As was the case with the toothpaste factory, my first six months in my new job, and even Wim Hof's experience, the why behind the buy drove the results.

While this book will now focus more on what happens after the why is uncovered, with hope, you understand the importance of its worth. Learn from my mistakes and the mistakes of others and try not to make assumptions without visiting the customer's workspace. Ask a lot of good open-ended questions to uncover the why and always track and adjust your thoughts in accordance with the customer's needs. Rest assured, the anchor can hold you down or set you free.

CHAPTER
Seven

MAP AND COMPASS

Planning and Prospecting Strategy

Elon Musk is many things: physicist, computer scientist, engineer, founder, co-founder, investor, billionaire. The list goes on and on. As a boy growing up in South Africa he was fascinated with computers and space. At the age of 12, when computers were still in their infancy, Musk constructed a game called Blaster that ran off 167 or so lines of code that he himself wrote. It earned him publication in a South African trade publication called *PC and Office Technology* and set the stage for Musk's future conquests.

With a combination of brilliance and creativity, Musk learned at a very early age that nearly anything could be mastered through its deconstruction and imaginative retooling. Hard work, planning, and perseverance could propel one to greatness. To him the only impediment to mastery was time. If he had the interest and time, he could do anything.

Today, as he sits perched atop the proverbial capitalist food chain as CEO/founder and Co-founder of Tesla and SpaceX, he gets a lot of attention. Often times we see Musk's name tied to extravagant and sometimes unflattering media appearances and publications. Seemingly he would be the type of guy who would be hard to work for and even harder to understand. At times his employees turn on him, and the critics pounce and trash his leadership and decision making. Why? Well, because no one roots for individuals to succeed at the expense of others and most understand you can't succeed without help. Yet, his businesses continue to grow and prosper despite headwinds and adversity.

Influence comes with vision, planning, clear messaging, and an understanding of human behavior. When the human behavior goes against an individual's decisions, then there often isn't enough hard work or brilliance to overcome it. No one, Musk included, can achieve greatness without the help and involvement of others. If one wants his or her ideas and businesses to change the world, he or she has to influence others. With that in mind, given Musk's long track record of success, one must assume he has mastered selling as well.

So then how does he do it? What can we learn from the master salesman? Well, as with most things, perhaps the best examples come with the learnings of failure. Imagine trying to sell something to Elon. What kind of preparation and planning would it take?

In Musk's biography, author Ashlee Vance, tells a story of a sales encounter one young salesman had with Musk. As Elon put it, "this guy was hounding me for a year with emails, publications, and data in an effort to get a meeting with me." Meetings with Musk were hard to get on the calendar, but this guy was relentless. For Elon, time is of the utmost importance and he doesn't simply meet with everyone that might have a product or service that would benefit him. Eventually, though, the concepts and products offered resonated with Musk, and he finally decided to take the meeting.

The meeting was to take place in Musk's office under a strict one-hour time frame, and the gentleman was to fly into New York for the meeting. It's the kind of meeting salespeople prepare their whole life for, but it lasted all of about two minutes. "The guy shows up and says he wants to get to know my business and build a relationship?" Elon's reply,

"Ok. Well, nice to meet you then," and sent the guy packing. He just couldn't believe the guy spent a year of his life trying to get a meeting and didn't come prepared with the knowledge of knowing exactly how he could help his business. Elon didn't have time to explain how the gentleman could help him and he certainly wasn't looking for more friends. It was a brutal reminder that value is what sells not relationships and it was a costly mistake for the salesman.

It might sound harsh, but there is a lot of truth and a lot to be learned from this encounter. Too often we don't spend enough time on planning and preparation in an effort to come ready to offer value. While we might not have sales meetings on the regular with the Elon Musk's of the world, everyone views time as a valuable commodity and they don't want it wasted.

A lot can be done ahead of meetings with doctors, business owners, customers, and even target markets prior to the sales encounter itself. Not everyone in your area is a good customer. In a sense you have to understand who you can provide the most value to. Planning and preparation of your strategy requires a lot of mapping. Prospecting requires the use of a compass to make adjustments along the way.

First let's address analyzing your territory itself by looking at probability and statistical analysis. Then we'll address prospecting through the lens of adjustment. You will learn about Bayes theorem, the Pareto Law (The Golden Rule), bucketing, routing, funneling, and scheduling.

Planning with a Map

Mapping your business is important whether you're new to a territory or market segment, or have years of experience with your customer base. It's an exercise that should be done with regularity and consistency. Benchmarks provide information and should be consistently monitored. The goal of mapping your current state is to gain an understanding of where you're getting your business, who from, and what opportunities or threats may exist within it.

Bucketing Your Business

Start by bucketing your business into three categories. Make a list of all your customers. Then do some analysis to understand what percent of your business comes from each.

Step one in this exercise is to decide which group of customers provides consistent and sustainable revenue. Call this group your "why" bucket because chances are, you're already aligned on value. Your why bucket will get plugged in later in routing and frequency, but for now just gain an understanding of who they are.

The next group should be customers who seemingly purchase with some regularity but are still inconsistent and ripe with potential. This is your "how" group. With a fuller understanding as to why their purchasing behavior is inconsistent and how to better align with their values and needs, you can theoretically see these customers as potential growth opportunities.

Lastly, take the remaining customers and label them your "what" group. Your what group has trialed or ordered a few times, but they are either early in development or you've yet to gain their trust and commitment at all.

The Golden Rule – Pareto's Law

After grouping your customers into the three segments and assigning revenue values to all of them, it's time to apply Pareto's Law. Pareto's Law states that roughly 80 percent of effects come from 20 percent of causes. It works with almost everything in life, including sales, and it's nearly impossible to change. In fact, you don't want to fight changing it, but instead understand how to apply it. Many sales organization and salespeople waste a ton of time, talent, and energy trying to fight this. They want every customer called on and ordering. They spend a ton of energy on trying to change the stack ranks with worthless incentives aimed at moving everyone at the bottom to the middle, and the middle to the top. The fact is even the stack ranks themselves, always, and I mean always, fit the golden rule. Just for fun, after you put this book down, take your company's stack ranks and see what percent of the sales growth in the company came out of the top 20 percent of salespeople. You will be shocked how close that number is to 80 percent.

Once you have found your top 20 percent of customers, make sure you do some analysis, possibly even asking them some questions with the hope of trying to understand how and why they are such good customers. Later we will talk about how to try to get new goals for the top 20 percent, and we'll also discuss how to keep your funnel full of new top 20 percent customers as competition or sales cycling removes a few from your pipeline.

Bayes' Theorem

Another common problem in sales organizations and amongst salespeople is a reliance on benchmark data to make inferences on future outcomes. Famous economists and psychologists, Daniel Kahneman and Amos Tversky, developed theories and statistics around such decision making. In fact, in 2002, Kahneman won a Nobel Prize for his work on prospect theory.

Prospect theory uses statistical analysis to use base rates in conjunction with probability and facts to assess the likely outcomes of event. It stems from Bayes theorem, developed much earlier by Reverend Thomas Bayes, in which statistical inference and probability is suggested to change when accounting for the availability of related evidence. To put it simply, decisions should be made off prior outcomes in conjunction with new evidence.

However, in sales, prior outcomes often far outweigh people's decisions. Let's look at an example, and then learn how to apply the practice in our planning and prospecting. When you have analyzed your top 20 percent and bottom 80 percent, look to find evidence supporting what placed the customers in either of the two buckets. Are there things that can be replicated to produce other similar outcomes? Was it windfall business, or was it driven by an approach? Say you have five customers in the top 20 percent, all with similar revenue and results. Two of the customers came from outside the territory, and the background on what drove the result is relatively unknown. The other three, however, all share similar traits. They all started trialing one of your products and slowly adopted the whole suite of products because of trust and knowledge in what the company's products had to offer. In all three cases these customers went from trialing to full adoption over a period of nine months. Thus, you know it's unlikely that a new customer now trialing your product will move much faster through this sales cycle given the same principles applying.

With this knowledge you shouldn't make projections of revenue equal to or exceeding the other customers like them in the upcoming two quarters. Therefore, any projection of sales revenue that doesn't align with the current state and past base rates should be re-evaluated.

Simply put, understanding what caused the current sales trends in your top 20 percent is important, but the true value is gleaning the evidence that supports replication and scale. When you're mapping out your revenue and predictions try to break down the territory and customer segmentation in a way that allows you to understand base rates in addition to new evidence. Place value on evidence found to improve outcomes and try to take emotion out of decision making. This will not only help you target better customers, but it will also help in planning your approach to them.

Prospecting with a Compass

Prospecting, much like planning, should be approached in a similar way. Don't spend too much time on prospecting dead ends. In order to do so, you have to have a good understanding of what and who is likely to achieve results. Everything from your planning, prospecting, targeting, and routing should account for evidence gathered and learned from your customer segmentation and territory alignment. We will talk more on targeting in the next chapter, but for now understand the application of this approach as it relates to your planning and prospecting. We will now begin to apply this in our approach to your day-to-day activities of routing, scheduling, and customer funneling.

Routing – Go the Way the Crow Flies

A quick analysis of top salespeople will show you they have their routing down to a science. Why? Working smarter is often more rewarding to your business than working harder. These top salespeople are effective, at least in part, because of the efficiency and frequency that's strategically planned. Look at routing as a map with a built-in compass for directional clustering. It vastly cuts down on the amount of time navigating takes. The goal, after all, isn't miles driven or the time logged, but instead efficiency on the path towards efficacy.

Let's break this down further. What is viewed by most people as a busy day isn't exactly that productive when we look more closely. It just feels like it because it's unorganized. Still these "busy days" are often filled with inefficiency and wasted time. Putting more constraints on your time can lead to real productivity. You can fit more on your plate if you make room and batch and que your work. I've found that working mothers in particular are good at this.

The first tip in routing is to realize this. Try an experiment. Force yourself to shorten your workday by four hours over a two-week period. When possible, do your work early and leave the afternoon open for planning and non-work-related tasks. Prepare at least one week in advance to allow yourself enough time to schedule productive meetings based off your territory analysis. For most sales jobs, two truly well planned and scheduled meetings a day will produce far more results than you're used to seeing. Route your additional calls needed around these two important meetings. These could be stop-ins or checkup meetings, but make sure they are close in proximity to the two scheduled ones.

Then, after the two weeks are up, look back and analyze your output. Were you able to be successful and productive with four hours less per day? How did it feel being prepared and more organized? Did you have success in the two meetings that were of the utmost importance? If you like the outcome, then all you need to do is expand upon it.

Funneling

It's important to look at prospecting as a funnel, but not in the sense you've perhaps looked at funnels in the past. The average or below-average sales reps constantly fill the top of their funnel and hope sales flush out at the bottom. Most top sales reps, however, analyze their business first and look for the best prospects to enter into the sales cycle. Based on attributes they have culled from analysis they can usually predict with fairly good accuracy the type of customers who will flush out results. Their funnel looks much more like a stock portfolio than an excel spreadsheet. It's full and diversified, and should it get too heavily weighted in one category or another, they simply adjust with a new stock that replaces what is missing. Every territory needs to have the long-term commodity stocks, the short-term high risk/high gain stocks, and low risk high reward long term stocks.

The exercises you did with Pareto's law and Bayes' theorem should help you pick customers that fit this mold to add into the funnel. Think of your why bucket as your commodity stocks, your how bucket as your short-term stocks, and your what bucket as your long-term stocks. If you are short on any and your customer portfolio gets out of balance, then you know where to spend your time prospecting.

Calendar and Schedule

Your calendar and schedule are what will separate your success in achieving good planning and prospecting. The most important things to get on your calendar, and keep on your calendar in the weeks ahead, are your two most important meetings of each day. When looking ahead a couple weeks or months, if you don't see these meetings scheduled yet, then you should start getting anxious. Instead of using that anxiety to be hard on yourself, let it drive you to fixing the problem. Then and only then start scheduling or filling in your calendar with appointments of less importance that are in a similar geography to your key ones.

Putting It All Together

With hope you now understand why master salespeople like Elon Musk have little patience for poor planning. Your map and compass give you direction and flexibility that will drive results and make you feel more prepared. To summarize it's as simple as understanding what your business looks like now, where you want it to go, and what you intend it to look like in the future. Use baseline data and real evidence to make your decisions and try to avoid emotion. If you find you can't make decisions without emotion, then devise a simple weighted algorithm to choose your targets and prospects. Assign equally weighted values to key attributes of successful customer profiles and then grade your prospects. Schedule your key meetings weeks and months in advance and then route your additional calls in accordance to the geography of these appointments. Constantly view your pipeline in terms of a stock portfolio and adjust your planning and prospecting according to need. By doing so you will find success in measurable ways you never thought possible!

CHAPTER
Eight

TARGETING WITH THE CANNONBALL APPROACH

Targeting Strategy in a Business Mindset

It was August 17, 2000, and Laird Hamilton was about to make history on what would later be dubbed the "millennium wave". Others had certainly done it, but Laird was about to perfect what later became known as tow surfing. In tow surfing, thrill-seeking ocean aficionados have small boats or jet skis drag them in line to catch the biggest waves. On this particular morning, Laird patiently waited and watched the surf as the swells grew bigger and bigger. With a goal of riding the "unrideable" and his friend to tow him out, Laird grabbed the rope and put faith in his abilities and his friend as a massive wave approached. His buddy, Darrick Doerner, recalled that as he drove out to sea, "I almost told him. Don't let go of the rope, but when I looked back, he was gone." Laird looked down the two-story swell and began a decent into what was widely thought to be the heaviest wave ever ridden.

61

Others have ridden much taller waves since, but Laird forever changed the sport and his life with that single wave. Had he hesitated or second guessed his attempt, he might not only have missed out on history but killed himself. It was his confidence, commitment, training, and patience that propelled him and the sport on a single wave.

In sales, good targeting takes a similar approach. Most salespeople sell like the average surfer, though: they see a wave, surf a wave, and repeat with little thought. Ask Laird what propelled his career, and he'll likely tell you that it's commitment and patience. In Scott Carney's book, *What Doesn't Kill Us,* Laird tells Scott, "You have to wait your time, commit, and envision yourself all the way through. If you crash you can't fight the thrashing currents, but instead submit, relax, and wait for your opportunity to escape. When it comes, you then have all the energy to give it everything you have to escape." In much the same way, we often get close to a huge, career-changing sales opportunity before avoiding commitment out of fear. When we crash, we fight it tooth and nail, instead of patiently waiting for the opportunity to escape and try again.

Selling is one-part planning and one-part commitment. The problem: when most salespeople plan, they use a shotgun approach, trying to spray their message across their territory. If they do encounter an opportunity to close a huge win, they bail out too early or ignore it all together. Top salespeople use experience and commitment to patiently await a big wave. Then, like Laird, they pounce on it. Think of planning and prospecting as your navigation tools, and targeting, as your wave of a lifetime. When you see your target, it's time to *commit!*

But we're pirates here, not surfers, so instead of using a shotgun approach, let's look at how to approach targeting with a cannon. For a cannon to sink a big ship, you must plan your approach and be strategic with your shot. You also must know when you're close enough to sink your target, while understanding that, inevitably, in doing so, you take on some risk as well. With all that in mind, let's look at some pirate tips on target strategy!

Get Your Sails Moving and You're Plates Spinning

There is a point in any new voyage or venture where you wonder if you should turn back. However, often, the opportunity cost of doing so far outweighs the benefit of pursuit. When you start a new workout, do you see results quickly? Have you ever broken a bad habit? If so, wasn't it the negative thoughts that almost derailed your progress? What would have been the cost in that instance if you'd let the lack of progress or negative self-talk push you into quitting?

Being in sales isn't so different. There's a point where you have to lean on prior success or extreme confidence to keep going; otherwise you'd simply give up. The problem with giving up goes beyond the defeated feeling of having failed. In giving up, you most often choose to pursue lesser goals, adopt strategies different from those you've honed, and, frankly, waste a ton of time. Many settle on mediocrity because they've benchmarked "success" on some middle ground or around their prior lackluster set of "successes."

Once you get the sails moving and your plates spinning, it's time to find your inner Laird Hamilton and attack with confidence. It's time to push beyond that middle ground you see others settling for and those so-so victories of your past. But pushing beyond into new realms is hard, right? You'll know when these points hit because you will feel stressed and anxious, and you'll start questioning yourself. While continuing to push the proverbial boulder up the hill forever might be a wasted endeavor, you do need to learn to live with a certain amount of distress, embracing the uncertain and uncomfortable feelings and asking yourself some hard questions. What, if anything, has changed that has me questioning this opportunity? Does my initial evidence and strategy still support this selling endeavor? Am I questioning myself or listening to the questioning of others who have done far less research? If the answers reveal that nothing has dramatically changed, then the evidence still supports pursuing your goal no matter how challenging it might be. If the doubts continue or grow, then run the scenario by a more seasoned and experienced person in your field or a business mentor.

A word of caution, though: whatever you do, don't give up without thoroughly putting the work into developing self-awareness and doing self and external analysis. Double down on your efforts and prepare and plan even more for your presentations, meetings, and follow-ups. Use things like deadlines, the law of scarcity, and goal alignment to keep your momentum. Prepare to sink the ship because often it's the point when you were just about to bail out where things turn and start moving in the right direction.

Know When to Use a Cannon

After getting over your internal and external obstacles, it's time to use that cannon. You're close now. Your big win is in your sights. Laser you're focus now, doing everything in your power to avoid distractions. Force yourself to hyper-prioritize in these moments. If you need to put in more hours during these times, then by all means do so. Set expectations with your other customers, and even your loved ones, to allow yourself that extra time and effort. It's one thing to blow off other meetings and commitments, but it's another to simply make compromises and ask for more time. More often than not you can explain to your family that you're in "plate-spinning mode," and that once things settle down, you'll take some extra time off to recharge and make it up to them. Other customers will often be okay too if you explain and set proper expectations of when you will be in next and give them a timeline. The cannon approach to targeting strategy has less to do with how and more to do with what. What you need is laser focus because in the past this is what likely derailed such opportunities.

My favorite example of the cannonball strategy described here is the pursuit of a new job or career opportunity. Over the years I've had numerous people reach out trying to get often-sought-after medical sales jobs. They submit cover letters, resumes, follow-up, and can't seem to figure out why no one will give them a chance. Then one day they finally make a connection through their network and get an interview. They again call wanting to know how to prepare. Usually the conversation centers on what information is a must know, what they should expect, and how they can best prepare. Valid questions, sure, but based on the number of people who then get beat out in the interview a week later, my gut tells me they simply tried to do "just enough" to get the position.

Enough is a hindsight, not a foresight, way of being. What you really need to do is reframe your mind. Top medical salespeople stay an average of five years in their new role and make in excess of $200,000 a year. What if someone told you they would give the person who could beat out five others to present on a certain topic $1,000,000 dollars as a reward next Friday? With a million on the line, how would you prepare? Would you wonder if you had done enough, or would you push to *know* you had done all you could? Go big and use a cannon when your next opportunity gets close, and you won't be left wasting time and wondering if you did enough.

Embrace Crashes and Misses

All good captains and salesman have crashes and misses on a number of close encounters. It's inevitable. And, yes, it hurts far worse when you can smell the victory only to watch it slip away.

However, even Laird Hamilton knew he would crash from time to time and had a plan for it. Should he crash on a 20-foot-plus wave, he knew it was again time to be patient and focus. As he explained to Carney when talking about crashing, "you have to slow your heartbeat when every cell in your body is telling you to freak out. Holding your breath requires the precious reserve of whatever oxygen remains in your red blood cells and calmness extends that. You can't fight yourself or the currents, you just have to calmly wait and watch for your exit. Then when the opportunity for exit arrives you give it all you got and fight for your life to scratch and claw back to the surface."

Similarly, when the cannons miss their mark, you can't panic and disregard your past experiences. Often people will fight a big loss only to later realize they were fighting themselves. Did you maybe need to just learn from a mistake and patiently go back to your approach? Or was it a worthy endeavor to make every excuse in the book to anyone and everyone who would listen as to why this or that didn't happen? Don't ignore self-analysis when you lose, but try to remove as much emotion from it as possible. Glean insight on only what can be done differently in the future, ignoring the rest.

Putting It All Together

When it comes to targeting, less is more, and strategy trumps all else. Start by casting a wide net and get as many plates spinning as possible. Force yourself to focus not on what's right in front of you, but what's likely to provide the desired result. Consider Laird Hamilton. He doesn't ride the first wave that comes his way. He analyzes the landscape and awaits the best opportunity. You should do the same.

And remember: benchmark not on what others would or have achieved in similar waters, but instead on your own vision and goals.

When the time is right, be prepared to go all in, and don't worry if you have some crashes along the way. You will crash. And every time you do, you will learn something that will better help you achieve that goal you're fighting towards.

Lastly, understand that targeting is a strategy, not a check-the-box formality. No one should know your business better than you so avoid any distraction that will derail your vision. Pick your wave and ride it!

CHAPTER

Nine

SAILS AND OARS

Decision Making Using Both of Your Systems

As mentioned earlier, Daniel Kahneman is the thought leader on the "think fast and slow" front. Simply using your gut alone, without prior experience, to make decisions can be dangerous. When your forced to make a decision quickly, sometimes your only choice is gut reaction, but the rest of the time you'll be best served to interject statistics. In fact, whenever possible, and on justified opportunities, rely on statistical analysis in conjunction with intuition.

Kahneman explains it as two systems. System one being the intuitive, unconscious, emotional, and automatic system where gut is in play. System two, therefore, is the opposite: slow, analytical, deliberate, and rational. Just using one system leads to misjudgment and error. Tie them together, and you get brilliance.

SYSTEM 1: THE SAILS – THINK FAST: USING YOUR INTUITIONS

The Logic and Benefit of Your Gut

We hear it all the time, and often from reliable sources, "trust your gut." But is it your gut or a deeper level of intuition? My whole life I've believed that the best decisions were made off a "gut" feeling and that the heart can lead you astray. We all know the story of the person who didn't do "this" or "that" because of some gut feeling and missed an opportunity. And then there's the story of the man who didn't get on the plane and it crashed. The point: whether the results end well or end poorly, gut intuition plays a big role in our everyday decision making.

The question becomes, should you always trust it? As it turns out that simple advice given by so many, to go with your gut, is anything but simple. Psychologists and scientists have studied the link between that "feeling" we get in our gut and those connections in our brain for years. Reading about this, you'll find that the stomach is a pretty amazing organ. In fact, it's the only other organ in the body with its own independent nervous system! The wall of our stomach is made up of a 100 million neurons that transmit signals and release chemicals directly to the brain. Think of it as a sophisticated system of algorithms that allow the brain to quickly do a Google search of a lifetime of experiences and exposure. The challenge: knowing when to trust these feelings, and even more importantly, when to trust someone else's over yours.

Here are five questions to ask that may help when deciding whether to go with your gut.

Is the gut feeling based on fact or fiction?

If we are all honest with ourselves, even the best "gut" decision makers have gotten it wrong a time or two. Remember the co-worker or classmate who you judged completely wrong? Or the career decision that you completely flopped on? Often this was made with that same intuition. These preconceived notions, though, were based on what you believed to be true, not on fact itself. Good intuition, gut feelings included, should still be based on experience and knowledge.

Has the gut feeling been put to the test?

Those who claim to be good at making decisions and use intuition to their advantage may very well live up to the hype, but they also likely have a lot of prior experience. Poker players, CEOs, and even psychics are good at their craft because of a lot of experience, past failures, and practice. In general, it may be a bad idea to make an important decision based solely on your gut feeling if you don't have any experience to go off of.

Am I better served to trust someone else's gut on this one?

If your gut is all you have to go off and you don't have any fact or experience to base your choice on, then what are you to do? The logical next step is to see if you can find someone else close to the situation who you trust and who may have some experience here. Ask them what their gut feeling is. The challenge is finding the right person for the situation.

How and why is emotion being removed here?

Some decisions may require evaluating why you are eliminating feelings of the heart. The "feelers" of the world often see the implications of the whole pie, meaning while the decision may be right for you, it may come at a price too high to pay for your family or others close to the decision. Simply put: if you know you aren't a feeler, or even if you think you are and you plan to make a decision that implicitly has emotions tied to it, take some time to double check and evaluate all parties involved. How will the decisions impact the others involved? While removing your own emotions from decisions is often helpful, you still must consider the emotional toll and impact it may have on others. While I realize this sounds like common sense and simple, it's often in hindsight that we realize this mistake. So, if you are going to make decisions correctly, choices with your sails and oars, then consider how they will affect your whole crew.

Have I given the decision enough time to evolve?

When in doubt, give it a day or two if you can. Science shows that sleep, nutrients, and bacteria in the stomach are constantly changing and turning on and off those 100 million neurons. Those neurons then release varying levels of important decision-making chemicals to the brain. This explains why a good night's sleep and a full belly can completely change your outlook.

SYSTEM TWO: THE OARS – THINK SLOW: ANALYTICAL ANALYSIS

System two is your analytical process. If you've ever labored over a decision and all the implications it carries, then chances are you have some experience with system two. The challenge is most of us infuse emotion in the wrong place and mistakenly attribute it to intuition, then allowing it to cloud our judgement. By eliminating emotions whenever possible and using statistics to back up your decisions, you'll often times get things right.

Let's do an example for fun. Let's say you win tickets to the show "The Price Is Right." As a lifelong fan of the show you have seen countless episodes, and your dream has always been to have your name called. Even though you realize the chances you'll play are slim, you decide to study up on the costs associated with various products from past episodes. The day of the show you review a list of prices in your pocket and anxiously hold your breath as they begin to call names. Just before the first name is called you get a weird feeling that today is your lucky day. And, sure enough, "come on down Richard Tyler Menke (yes I was born a dick)" is called out.

Now, the first fallacy is that you will likely tell people about that feeling as if it was intuition. However, the number of other people who had that same feeling and weren't called statically trumps your result. Given you have no experience guiding this intuition and others had the same feeling and didn't have their name called, what just happened was likely dumb luck.

Then comes intuition fail number two, and this time it's more costly. The first item up for bid is a recliner. The first contestant bids $1,750. The second $1,999. The third $1,450. Now it's your turn. You can't remember seeing the past prices on this item and your gut is telling you it can't be as high as some of these bids.

Statistically your best bet is to bid one dollar more than the highest bidder. This is because, in the history of the game show, imploring this strategy would result in a 54 percent chance of winning. Although, in reality, contestants often get swayed by the audience or intuition and end picking a different tactic. They allow influence to weasel its way into and over their own emotions. The result? Over the history of the show the actual last bidder only wins 34 percent of the time. A stark contrast to the 54 percent opportunity available to those willing to simply bid one dollar more than the highest bid.

So there you stand, shaking on the inside, as the audience yells and your gut screams that it's closer to $1,700. Thus, you inexplicably blurt out $1,700. Now, obviously, your first mistake was the perplexity of this bid itself. If you thought it was closer to $1,700 and the bids on either side of this were $1,450 and $1,750 you could have bid $1,451, giving yourself a much wider range to be right and still honoring your gut.

The second failure was again not looking at the statistics. If you truly thought the bids were high and had no idea on the actual price, then bidding one dollar would have been your second-best choice.

Then the moment culminates. Bob (I'll say Bob because it's just not the same with Drew Carey) then calls out...dun dun dun... "the actual retail price is.... $1,499." Your head lowers. Your heart sinks. And you head back to your seat. You remove the price sheet from your pocket, and you see that in fact you did have the recliner on there and it had previously bid at a retail price of $1,450.

Now on statistics alone you should have bid $2,000 dollars, in which case you would have lost. The reason being is that since game participants must choose "the closest price without going over," it leads people to often under bid. By doing so, peoples' guesses disproportionately skew the range, thus making the choice of one dollar over the highest bid a slightly better option than the bid of a dollar itself.

However, you being the Price is Right scholar you are, knew in this case the bids were high. Therefore, statistically, your second-best choice should have been one dollar. But maybe you never thought it was lower than $1,450, which was the lowest bid. Your gut was indeed saying $1,700. Your knowledge of the show and past pricing couldn't consciously remember exact prices, but knew it wasn't less than $1,450.

So, all things considered, and in this instance, had you combined your intuition with statistical analysis you would have landed on range three and bid $1,451. This being the third biggest range, and the one inclusive of your gut feeling amount of $1,700. Furthermore, had you combined the two models, that being your gut founded on experience, and your head focused on statistics, you would have won!

Unlike the intuition you thought you had when your name was called, your pricing intuition was founded on base rates and experience, thus it should have been considered. Yes, the intuition was deeply subconscious and non-specific, but it was based on experience. Experience that others likely didn't possess.

So, what are we to learn from this example? Two things. One: don't dismiss your intuitions, but don't make decisions based solely on them either. Two: don't make decisions based solely on statistics, but don't make important ones without analyzing them.

Think fast and slow as Daniel Kahneman teaches. Whenever possible, use both systems, in combination, conjunction, and perfect harmony.

Deciding Where to Spend Your Decision-Making Energy

But what if you have too many decisions to make and you start making bad ones in haste? Proper decision-making requires time and commitment. As the old saying goes, "you can't be everything to everyone," therefore decision making itself requires some analysis in an effort to prioritize. When trying to decide what and where to put your effort, there are some proven methods that will help: Prioritization on Value Seen by the Receiver, Using Simple Weighted Algorithms to eliminate emotion, and Looking for Waving White Flags. We will touch on them all in detail below.

Prioritize Based on the Value Seen in the Eyes of the Receiver

In his best-selling book, *The Twelve Rules of Life,* Jordan Peterson poetically and descriptively writes of the proverbial swings and misses of human nature. His second rule for life, "treat yourself like someone you are responsible for treating," hit home with me in more ways than one. As the oldest of five children and having grown up on a farm with an alcoholic father, I'd become a fixer by nature. Countless times I had tried to seek help or get help for my dad. When that proved a failure, all I wanted was to be there for my mom and help fix the pain I saw in my sibling's eyes caused by my dad's behaviors and choices.

As time went on, and seemingly with no acknowledgement, I began to start trying to fix everyone around me who looked like they needed help. My subconscious had seemingly been trying to correct things from my past that I felt I had failed at. Not only did I not know how to stop trying to fix things, I didn't even realize I was *trying* to fix things.

Unbeknown to me, though, a flaw had found its way into my logic. I hadn't yet realized that you can only help someone who wants to be helped. Human nature will accept whatever comes its way, but that doesn't mean you should forfeit your well-being without checking in on motive. Peterson uses the analogy of a dog, man's best friend. People will go to great lengths to make sure their beloved dog gets the best vet care, food, attention, etc. They will literally ignore their own health, hobble into the vet on one leg, swollen and bruised, to get heart worm shots for "Fido."

What is the reason behind this? Can it be that they literally see their four-legged friend as more deserving of health and happiness? The flaw of this of course is that the four-legged friend has become domesticated and dependent on this leg dragging bipedal caregiver. Should the caregiver go, then so to would the beloved pet.

Therefore, we must remain focused on those willing to be recipients of value. What plays out in the relationship described above also plays out routinely in the business world. If you think for a second your time isn't deserving or that your value isn't worthy, then how can you earn the respect of those around you? If you want to make decisions on whom to first help, ask yourself if the receiver sees value in what you have to offer. Who is most willing to be accepting of what you have and truly want the help and value you bring? Prioritize based on the value seen in the eyes of the receiver themselves.

Use Simple Weighted Algorithms

In true Daniel Kahneman fashion, once you have focused on a pool of customers who see value in what you bring, it's time to apply statistics. Don't fret if you aren't an Excel spreadsheet or Gantt chart junkie. This can be simple. I'll use a couple examples to analyze this, but what it really comes down to is a set of variables with equally weighted values. The goal is to combine base rates, statistics of known significance, and all variables of knowledge and experience into an unemotional but rational formula. This can be applied to targets you're trying to funnel in or out of your top 20 percent. Furthermore, this system can be applied to entire territories, geographies, and even sales forces. The beauty of the fast and slow approach is that you avoid preconceived notions and biases while taking emotion out of the equation.

Ever listen to the commercials that financial advisors put out? They always say something to the effect of "we are here for you, when times get tough, let us take the guesswork out." What they are doing is harping on the fact they know emotions play into stock picking. Knowing this they believe that if you have ever been burnt stock picking, that chances are you will remove yourself from the equation and insert them. However, often times with a little planning and pre-work you can create these algorithms for yourself.

Example: Weighted Algorithm for Picking Your Targets

When you get to the spot where you have more potential targets than you know what to do with, it's time to implore strategy. It's always a good problem to have when we get to a place when our messaging has landed us more prospects than we can feasibly pull through. That being said, none of us are likely to be able to effectively pull them all through. Furthermore, the golden 80/20 rule has stood the test of time. As stated, you will get 80 percent output from 20 percent of your customers, so your best chance of success comes from picking the best of the best top 20 percent gainers. Imagine having the top salesperson from each of the top companies in your industry all on your team. What would the outcome be? If you could achieve this in your own territory, with your customer base, and have a similar outcome wouldn't it be worth the extra vetting work? Thus, spending a little more time upfront to get it right would seemingly be a worthy endeavor. So, give it a shot!

Setup

Take your customer base and stack rank them on revenue generation from highest to lowest. Then on a separate tab or worksheet rank them on perceived potential. Finally, on a third sheet, come up with a list of variables that you believe will increase or decrease their ability to take action or implement change. For each of these factors assign an equally weighted value. For instance, let's say the factors are "red tape," "readiness," "purchasing power," and "internal influence." On your first two spreadsheets each of your customers are stack ranked and each sheet has a .25 value since there are two factors (current revenue and potential revenue). Your third spreadsheet is then worth the remaining .5 value and is stacked ranked on the variables you assigned. For each variable use a value from 1 thru 10 for each customer (1 being they are high in that variable and 10 being they are low). Then run a sum function and stack rank your third sheet from lowest value to highest. In this example, the lower the value, the higher they are in all four variables. Finally write a formula such that X=sheet1 rank times .25 + sheet2 rank times .25 + sheet3 rank times .5. The resulting list will then rank your customers from top to bottom based on current revenue + potential + knowledge. By doing this you have done something similar to what most stockbrokers do. You have reduced, but not eliminated personal knowledge and emotion. The formulas and spreadsheets depicting this example, along with a free tool you can use for your own customer base, can be found in the index or online at www.thepirateguides.com.

Booty Abound—Be on the Lookout for Waving White Flags

When you think of a waving white flag, you think of surrender. While no customers are likely to wave white flags, you certainly can uncover low-hanging fruit with a little analysis. Typically, there are three factors that will attribute to easy targets. The first is identification of a change.

Imagine you're in Vegas betting on the Men's NCAA tourney. With more teams and variables, and less betting to tip off the oddsmakers, there are inconsistencies to be found in the numbers. For instance, let's say in talking with a friend from home you uncover that the local news has mentioned a star player has now been ruled out from a broken leg in morning practice. The line seemingly still shows that the odds makers haven't heard this same news, and the betting isn't high enough to tip off a change. Originally you had intended on putting 100 dollars on each of three games you did research on. However, knowing this new information, and seeing an inconsistency, you decide that instead of betting on three different games with the 100 dollars, you will instead put it all on this one game and take the spread. The game ends up being a blowout with the underdog winning and you come out victorious.

The second thing to look for when searching for low-hanging fruit is a lack of competition. Like the NCAA games, if the sheer volume doesn't exist, then there should be less data to support what had previously been thought. Rural communities, companies that have changed decision makers or business models, and targets with strong gatekeepers are often good examples of this. A strong gatekeeper can sometimes be circumvented, and once you do, then you know that same person will keep the other competition out. Often you might find that once you have crossed the mote that previously secured the castle, that the doors are wide open.

The last sign of a white flag is a new market entry. Never ignore new business that pops up from a customer you have never heard of previously. Sometimes this is a sign of influence from the outside and you only have so much time to sure up this windfall business.

Putting It All Together

Once you have identified where to spend your time, remember the principles of the sail and oars and use both. What is your gut reaction and can you trust it? Do you have another contact, mentor, or friend who you could bounce the idea off? Lastly, how can you eliminate emotion from the decision and analyze the situation with statistics? Can you use a simple weighted algorithm or baseline data to create analysis? Remember that we have two systems for a reason. Combine your baseline experiences with statistical analysis. Think in terms of the "Price Is Right" scenario and find ways to combine your gut with data. By putting it all together, you will navigate the waters ahead with ease and efficiency.

CHAPTER
Ten

TAKE THE HELM

Opening with Empathy, Transparency, and Brutal Honesty

Okay. Take a deep breath! We are halfway through our journey together and have yet to really dive into the sale itself. In some regards, this is purposeful, as at least half, if not more, of selling is preparation. And trust me when I say this: we all could do more of it. Having worked with hundreds of other reps in the field, I'm always struck by how little preparation most of us put into selling. It's as if we all have so much confidence in ourselves and our abilities that we honestly believe we can wing it to some degree. Sure, we prepare on some things, but on others we make assumptions. And we know what they say about assumptions.

The more attention to detail you invest, the more smoothly the next part (the sale itself) will go. With hope you have found some gold and treasure in these stories and insights shared so far. With any luck, these insights will now build into actionable sales techniques as we approach Part Two: The Points of Sail.

From here on we will focus on the sale itself, starting with the ever-important opening of the sales call. In the rest of the book you'll hear less from leading experts and more from other top salespeople across the country. Additionally, the second half of the book will give you a framework for selling differently. Will all the concepts require a shift in approach for you? Probably not. Are they all new concepts? Definitely not. However, there is a purposeful and proven strategy in the sequence and methods laid out here. While it will take practice and effort to make it your own, the process will enable you to sell effectively in any industry, environment, and time allotment.

Stepping into the Waters: What Makes a Good Opener?

It was spring break 2002, and I wanted to go to Panama City, Florida with a group of friends. As the oldest child, I did not have the privilege of learning from my older siblings as to how I would pitch this proposition. However, one thing I knew for sure was that I would need to change my perspective. I put myself in my parent's shoes. What were they going to fear? What influence did other parents have on them if any? What would minimize their fear if they let me go? What benefit, if any, did they stand to gain from giving me this freedom? Thinking in this way allowed me to envision, plan, and practice so that when the real talk went down, I was already armed with thoughtful and empathetic responses.

Here's the crazy part. They actually let me go. I nailed the sale. The odd thing is that petulant teenagers often do get this negotiation right. No that doesn't mean they all convince their parents to let them go, but chances are they had some impact or influence. Why? Because they prepared from the vantage point of their parent's lenses, versus their own. The takeaway: if we all approached sales like we did when planned to ask our parents for something preposterous during our youth, chances are we would see a lot more results.

The key to a good opener is to let the other party know you're on their side. Your goal is to quickly diffuse preconceived notions and gain trust, credibility, and impact. In interviewing numerous top salespeople for this book and in general observation, there are three great approaches that we will cover for doing this.

The Ricky Roma of Opening

When I began my research on opening, I immediately thought of my old college roommate, Aaron Wozniak. We are all familiar with the "closer." The guy or gal who sales movies like "Glengarry Glen Ross" and "Wall Street" were made for. They come in and get people to hand over their money with force and finesse.

In the real world, though, closing doesn't work like this anymore. No longer do we feel obligated or pressured to buy, and if we do, we certainly won't repeat the experience. Opening is the new closing, and Aaron is the Ricky Roma of opening.

I asked Aaron what makes a good opening to a sales pitch or presentation. His reply, "win their hearts in the first five seconds." To Aaron, selling isn't a game or even a skill, it's an honor. He gets to bring new solutions and ideas to the companies he works for and the providers he works with. When I approached him about inclusion in this book, he was hesitant. Not because he didn't want to be misrepresented, but instead, like me, he wasn't sure he even wanted to be lumped into a category of a "sales guy," especially when so many do it poorly. The reality is all good salespeople feel this way at some point because they can't be categorized and tend to be innovators on more levels than one.

He understands the value and opportunity that arises when great innovation is matched with an emotional gripping message. Not only does he take pride in the work he does, but more important to any label, salesman or otherwise, is the caring and charismatic approach he takes to being a problem solver. Thus, when I asked him to describe how he opens a sales pitch it was like pulling teeth from the mouth of a crocodile. Not only was he resistant to give me answers, he didn't seem to have a "go to" or "canned pitch." By my estimation and his this was because one doesn't exist. "You just have to do your research and truly understand things from the customer's point of view," Aaron said. However, after a lot of back and forth and the sharing of many examples, we did find commonality in approach.

When the dust settled, we landed on one goal for opening a call and three approaches that seemingly work if you want to achieve it. The goal of the opening is to grant yourself enough time, to win more time, as you build to the anchor, or the why. The way to achieve this is through gaining immediate trust and connection. Like most things, how you build trust and connection is unique to the personality. We did however agree on three tactics that we both have seen work time and time again.

Opening Tactic One: Empathy

Empathy is quite possibly one of the most underutilized and most powerful tools in your arsenal. However, it can't be effectively faked, or at least not in the way that most do it. In order for it to truly work you have to be able to map out the sales call in your head prior to the meeting, thinking of every possible feeling, fear, or doubt the other party might have. Ask yourself, how would I feel in their shoes? What do I know about these people's personality that will help alleviate their fear and uncertainty? What can I give them up front to help gain trust in guiding them to a new perspective? In this manner you aren't faking the empathy at all, but instead walking through it with them. In much the same way I discussed preparing to ask my parents to go on spring break, you absolutely must gain insight into their point of view. By doing so, it shows respect and creates a dialogue that allows for safe and open discussion on the most pressing issues. The goal of empathy then aligns perfectly with the goal of opening, which is to get more time. Start off on the wrong foot and you open yourself up to the possible outright answer of a flat no!

Opening Tactic Two: Transparent Selling

This brings us to the second key, transparency. When I say transparency, I don't mean showing up feeling like you are the underdog trying to win over Elon Musk. No, you still have to maintain the confidence and swagger that you belong there and toe a line of tension. What I do mean is transparency in a sense that you are prepared in a number of ways and unclear in others. You feel strongly that you can help them but may want guidance on where.

Doing this isn't as simple as Googling their credentials or trying to learn their interests and hobbies from Facebook. Instead, what you want to portray is that you have prepared from their vantage point. Again, think of this in terms of the negotiation of the spring break trip. Preparing in this way allows you to become mobile and tactile; ready to change colors like a chameleon and stay one step ahead of the objection.

Transparency allows you to lay the objections out on the table and create dialogue. In some instances, you'll speed up the call by handling objections prior to them even being brought up, and in others, you'll uncover things that you didn't know would impede progress. Either way you are laying it all out on the table, and that is how you want to open!

Opening Tactic Three: Brutal Honesty

Maybe you don't display it now, but as a kid you were likely the "king" of brutal honesty. Your inquisitive nature led you to question everything and say it out loud. Sure, most of this showed your lack of emotional intelligence that would later need to be tempered, but there was a *huge* benefit to those years when you could just say and ask anything! What benefit was that? If you think about it, the "sponge effect" so often spoken of, was a direct result of a lot of direct questions and comments that led to immediate answers and responses. There was no "beating around the bush" as a kid and when you were in that environment of learning the world allowed you a lot of free passes. So how do you create this environment as an adult without offending anyone? Or better yet have it viewed as refreshing? The answer is to put it all out there.

When you plan your presentation or pitch, think of your audience and how they will likely view *you*! Whether they know you or not, if you haven't been brutally honest with them then the trust just isn't there. Trust is number one in buying, so you better get this right from word one in selling. Look at all the objections that are likely to impede progress and grant your customers to be right on a few! An opener like, "Look (enter doc, sir, ma'am), I realize people come in all the time pitching all sorts of things. I'm someone who is honest in my approach, and I don't want to waste your time. My hope is that you are the same and will treat me similarly. In researching your business I've identified a few ways I think I can help. Some of the stuff we sell adds absolutely no value to your business currently and thus, unlike the suits before me, I've cut it from this presentation. If at any point I cover something that doesn't apply to you, or your business, feel free to stop me."

Whatever you say after this, make sure you set yourself up for a productive back and forth and separate yourself from the rest of the pack. The goal is a foundation set on mutual trust. Don't treat brutal honesty in the same emotionally unintelligent way you did as a child, but also don't be afraid to set up a little candid conversation. By doing this you grant the other party authority to say what they are actually thinking which often times isn't bad. If you can handle objections in person rather than in email or post call follow-up, then you are far more likely to speed up the selling process.

Putting It All Together

Again, when it comes to opening, your goal is to have the other party believe you are on their side. Remember the words of my old college roommate Aaron and "win them over in the first five seconds." When I heard Aaron say this, I was reminded of a story of my late father that perfectly highlights the approach. My dad was the master at this immediate connection and after his passing, a group of his friends shared a story that perfectly explains how you want to approach opening.

As the story goes, my dad and his friends were out to dinner in the early 90s at the height of the Red's "Nasty Boys" dynasty. Spotting several of the World Series-bound Cincinnati Reds' players eating with their wives in a restaurant in Northern Kentucky, my dad, knowing his two young boys at home were fans, wanted to approach the table for a picture and an autograph. His friends pleaded to leave the men be and not make a scene. However, my dad could not be stopped. After a few minutes of sitting quietly at the table, my dad apparently stood up and quickly walked over to their table. Within minutes, as my father's friend Kevin explained, "he had the whole table laughing and clapping. They were all shaking hands and chumming it up like old buddies and we were all like 'what in the hell did he just do?"

As it turned out, what happened was nothing short of pure genius. My old man, knowing the Reds players likely got bombarded on the regular, knew he would have to do something different. He decided he would go over to the table and introduce himself first to the wives and ask for their autographs. The players, having seen plenty of awkward intros, thought this was hilarious.

"You sure you don't want our autographs?" asked Joe Oliver.

"Nah" said my dad, "You all sign plenty but your wives are clearly the better-looking half." Then, after a little back and forth they all got up and took a group picture that my dad later got signed. The picture, and memento to the 1990 World Series champs, still hangs in my weight room to this day, but the story of how it came to be had never been told.

So, you see when you come up with an opening try to be different and charismatic. Think, "What would others do here and how can I be different?" Harken back to your times as a kid and think in terms of the spring break scenario. How often could you convince your parents of something when you were a youngster just by understanding and even anticipating their thoughts? Could the same approach be used in your selling methods today?

Take control of the helm and the call, but in a subtle and strategic, captain-like manner. Empathy, transparency, and brutal honesty, when used in conjunction with planning and purpose, are great tools to get you off and sailing. Figure out which approach is likely to resonate with your audience. If you don't know ahead of time, it's worth making a phone call or two to other reps or employees that know the personality better. If all else fails then prepare as if they are you. We are all more similar than we think, and chances are if you approach them in a manner that you yourself would respect, then your message will hit home. Hell, maybe even Joe Oliver will be there to guide you into home.

CHAPTER
Eleven

VIEW FROM THE CROW'S NEST

The New Perspective

As a father of three, I'm constantly surprised by the amount of stuff I learn from my kids. Their insights and perspective often leave me questioning myself and that's rarely a bad thing. One of the situations that will often lead to these moments happens when I'm reading them childhood fairy tales. As a kid I can remember asking my mom question after question while listening to stories like *Pinocchio, The Beauty and The Beast, and Cinderella,* all of which are all chocked full of lessons for life and love.

Recently I was reading the enchanting stories of Ebenezer Scrooge to my oldest son, Jack. As had happened so many times before, I was struck by the insights of Dickens's famous tale. As most of you know, in the story Scrooge is visited during his dreams by three ghosts: the ghost of Christmas past, the ghost of Christmas present, and the ghost of Christmas yet to come. Scrooge, having spent most of his adult life compiling and counting his wealth, finds himself tortured in his dreams

84

of past, present, and future. In the first ghostly encounter, the ghost of Christmas past takes Scrooge on a journey back to his youth, where he sees a younger more innocent version of himself he can barely recognize. In the scene Scrooge is filled with sadness as he watches his young self from afar struggle to find his way in a lonely world. Having lost his dad, and his way, the ghost takes Scrooge on a journey to witness his then fiancé, Belle, leaving him after she realizes he will never love her like he loves his money. The scene concludes with Scrooge watching an adult Belle huddled around a Christmas tree with her huge, happy family as she recounts the frivolous nature of the death of Scrooge's business partner, Marley, who died without having experienced love.

In the next dream, Scrooge is visited by the ghost of Christmas present, who takes him on a journey through the night to visit the house of his employee, Bob Cratchit, whom Scrooge had just begrudgingly allowed to take Christmas Eve off in adherence with custom. As Scrooge watches from afar, the reader gets introduced to the iconic character of the story, Tiny Tim, the crippled son of Bob. The ghost informs Scrooge that Tiny Tim is so ill that he won't survive without the medical attention the family can't afford. Scrooge is then warned by the spirit that should he not help his own employees and their families that he will find himself dying a miserable man in much the same way Marley did.

In the last ghostly encounter, the spirit of Christmas yet to come visits as the story itself begins to take shape. During this visit, Scrooge is cast into a vision of the future, allowing him perspective into what his life will become should he not change his misguided ways. As the scene unfolds the spirit takes Scrooge on yet another journey. This time he is forced to bear witness to Bob Cratchit and his family as they mourn young Tiny Tim, who has died. This alone is tough for Scrooge to see. To make matters worse, the spirit then takes Scrooge to a dark and gloomy tombstone in a deserted graveyard where weeds and plants have overgrown a headstone that bears Scrooge's own name. It is at this point that Scrooge begs for forgiveness and vows to change his ways should he be allowed another chance. He then awakens from his night terrors a changed man. As the story concludes, Scrooge is shown nurturing little Tiny Tim back to health and helping aid all those he had neglected through the years.

The story, iconic in its own right, is not that unique in its lessons. Many of us struggle to understand the ways the past has shaped us, how the present affects us, and what the future holds. The story of Scrooge is one of shifting perspective that is deeply rooted in the "why." Scrooge's own childhood loneliness and challenges led him astray and perpetuated his pain when his attempts to mask that hurt with money fell short. On a lesser scale, the story is very much analogous to the importance of perspective as it relates to selling. Where are your customers coming from in their position on what you have to offer? What effect does their current situation have on them now? How might you cast a vision of the future in much the same way the ghost of Christmas yet to come did for Scrooge. Part two of the sale is framing this perspective in what we will call "the new view," or "the crow's nest perspective."

The Crow's Nest Perspective

After you've taken the helm and succeeded in getting the other party to believe you're on their side, it's time to start introducing a new perspective with a view from the crow's nest. In much the same way Scrooge was unable to see his own unhappiness, sometimes your customers can't see a path to a different or better way. Your goal in preparation should have been rooted in understanding their world and their influences. Therefore, all you are doing now is tailoring a new method or vehicle for achieving a future state that will enhance or improve upon their goals.

But doing this does takes insight. Here's the part of the sale where your research really starts to help. If you've done your preparation through prior sales calls, observation, and research, then you've learned a bit about what drives your customer or customers. Do they want improved efficiency or simply to differentiate from the competition? Are they seeking improved performance, or, as with doctors, improved outcomes? Do they value revenue generation over all else, or do they simply need what you have to offer as a way to check a box or fill a gap? Whatever the case, by knowing their situation, you'll know how to shift their perspective to meet what you're selling. It's as simple as explaining: "you are here on the map, and I want to get you over there!"

Tie to the Anchor

When it comes to perspective shifting, the trick is to always tie to the anchor; in other words, meet the customer's "why." No one has the time, energy, money, or even passion to change something that's working. It's easy to sell something day in and day out to those who need it, but how many potential customers do you have to run through to find the few who actually do? Changing perspective requires a reframe in mindset. It requires an understanding of what makes people tick, and most importantly, it requires an understanding of desire. On a lesser scale one might sell a new printer copier by only approaching customers on a list that shows old or outdated equipment. But what if the seller runs out of those customers and still needs to make sales? Aren't there likely companies that need better service, more reliability, or improved efficiency with their equipment, perks that would outweigh the benefit of a short term sunk cost?

To use another example more closely tied to my background, let's say you sell a device that helps doctors do a procedure that is minimally invasive. The list of hospitals that allow new vendors and have purchasing power is short in demand. However, you uncover that in the office setting the doctor could conceivably do the same procedure at less cost to the patient and with more reimbursement to them. The doctor, making enough money as is, shows no interest in changing something for more money, but you know that. You sell him on the benefit to the patient paying less and win him over.

Whatever the case may be, if you anchor the new perspective on the why, you're offering is likely to resonate, and that's enough to keep your pitch going! Think of it like bearing witness to the customer's "ghost of Christmas past." Like Scrooge, if you know where the customer is coming from, then you can tie in all the elements that will move the needle.

Once you have identified your anchor, there are three steps to take in your perspective shift or new view.

Let's start with the obvious.

Step 1: Starting from Their Perspective

As is the case with all of these steps, the level of detail here is dependent on your level of preparation. The level of preparation then is likely dependent on the type and length of the sales process in your industry. If you are in a faster-paced selling environment requiring a lot of targets, then maybe you didn't or don't have the time to do an actual observation prior to the sale. While I'll argue that in true business strategy you always want to spend a little more time on the potential targets that drive the 80/20 rule, not every customer fits that mold. If you did observation in your preparation then you'll know what perspective you are starting from here. What is the customer's world? Where can you provide them value? What slows their productivity, impedes their progress, or keeps them up at night? This is where you want to start. In much the same way the reader understood where Scrooge was coming from after the dream of the ghost of Christmas past, you need to understand where your customer is and start there. If you haven't done observation, then do research by calling other reps that know the customer. Look back at prior notes. Do some research on the industry online.

A helpful tool for analyzing perspective is the old-fashioned SWOT box. Draw a box up and cut it into four sections. Then use your research to write down the strengths, weaknesses, opportunities, and threats of your customer's business.

From this list then develop the first part of your crow's nest perspective, beginning with a statement that encompasses their current view.

Example 1: Doc, in spending some time prior to this meeting observing how you work up patients with X condition, it's become apparent to me that you face a number of challenges with this.

Example 2: Mr. or Mrs. Smith, in an attempt to make sure I understood your business a little better, I did some observation prior to this meeting with your employees using X piece of equipment. It would seemingly be the case that you have challenges with this.

Example 3: Having worked with other customers like you in the past, a lot of them tell me they have challenges with X. Is this the case with you?

Step 2: Flush Out Obstacles and Objections

Whatever real world scenario you just laid out is now likely to start a dialogue. Your potential customers will either agree with your assessment or disagree. Agreeability is the obvious goal, but if you find yourself in disagreement, then just fall on your sword, explain your intentions, and ask more questions. The purpose in finding agreeability is to understand as much as possible in the shortest amount of time as possible. Then you can flush out the obstacles and objections that are impeding progress. This is one part objection handling and one part perspective shifting. You aren't trying to handle every objection right now—if you were you might not get any further. Validate their concerns, understand their world, take notes, actively listen, and build on the areas where you currently agree. Here are some examples of language that builds on the prior step.

Example 1 (You): Doc, in spending some time prior to this meeting observing how you work up patients with X condition, it's become apparent to me that you face a number of challenges with this.

Example 1 (Customer Response): "Actually while we have challenges with that we struggle more trying to achieve (new objection.)"

Example 1 Response (You): "Interesting. That is helpful to know. Like I said, as much as I want to understand your business in an attempt to provide value, it's this kind of information that often I can't anticipate. I will see what I can do to address this. Let me do some research."

Example 2 (You): "Mr. or Mrs. Smith, in an attempt to make sure I understood your business a little better, I did some observation prior to this meeting with your employees using X piece of equipment. It would seemingly be the case that you have challenges with this?"

Response 2 (Customer Response): "Yes that's true, but what you sales reps never seem to realize is all the other stuff that makes fixing that impossible."

Example 2 Response (You): "Well you don't know me well enough to appreciate this yet, but I sincerely apologize that I hadn't come to that realization prior to this meeting. I pride myself in preparation so I can provide value. Will you explain a little more about the challenges? I work hard to find creative solutions and if you just explain a little further, I promise at the very least I will exhaust my resources in looking for solutions."

Example 3 (You): "Having worked with other customers like you in the past a lot of them tell me they have challenges with X. Is this the case with you?

Response 3 (Customer Response): "Yes that's true, but how can you help me with that? It's never been anything anyone has been able to address or help with in the past."

Example 3 Response (You): "I have some ideas that I believe will help, but if it's ok with you I'd like to keep digging into your business and then we can map out the ideas for all of it at the end?"

Step 3: Goal Alignment in the New Perspective

The true goal alignment will happen in step five in your value proposition, but now is a good time to check in to see if you are on track. What used to be called a trial close might be a little strong, but this is a similar concept. Based on the progress so far you want to mirror responses looking for the customer to say "that's right" or "yes." Once you have them aligning on a couple key points, ones that will tie into the value proposition, then you can grant yourself the right to move on to the next phase.

If you're struggling to get the response you want, find one area of agreeability and move on. Again, you don't want to spend all your time here handling objections, you just want to flush out the big ones that will impede progress and find a couple areas of agreeability that show alignment with their goals.

Putting It All Together

Remember the story of Scrooge when you're trying to plan and prepare your pitch. Develop a reframe and weave in a story that will help shift the perspective from the current state to the future. We can all relate to customers that very much resemble Scrooge, but everyone has a "why" behind their behaviors and actions. How many great future customers could we win over if we just spent a little more time understanding their current state and guide them to a path forward?

One such example of this comes to mind from my time selling GYN surgical devices. I was working in surgery with a doctor who was an avid user of our products when a tech from the room next door came over and asked if I could assist Dr. R with a procedure.

Having attempted to get time with this doctor before, I was perplexed by the request because she was not a fan. In fact, she seemed to hate reps in general and had never used any of our products. As it turned out, this bold surgical tech, recognizing the doctor needed some help with a more precise instrument, didn't even ask Dr. R if she wanted to try my product. He grabbed me and said, "Listen Tyler. We all know Dr. R can be cranky, but she's not gonna finish this case unless she uses a more powerful and precise morcellator.

"I told her you were here, and she said to put your stuff on standby, but she has yet to say she would use it. Go in there and tread carefully and work your magic."

Work my magic, I thought? *She's gonna kick me out of there and chew me up faster than the device I brought in could!*

However, despite my fear, I accepted the challenge. I came in and said, "Dr. R, Tyler here. I finished up a case next door, and it's my understanding you've got quite the challenging case here. For the sake of time, I'm going to quietly set up behind you, just in case. My hope is you will complete this surgery without needing any further frustration, but the last thing I'd want is to not be prepared for you and your patient should you need it."

Her response? Crickets. She said nothing, as if I was a ghost. Okay, I thought, well she didn't say no or kick me out, so I'm going to do as I said and start getting things and people in order. Once the techs had the equipment ready, I sat and observed the monitors and watched her work. I was looking for an opportunity to interject with anything of value. It was then I noticed that the fibroid she was working on was extremely calcified at the base. "Boy," I said, "I've been in 100s of myomectomy cases this month and have yet to see a fibroid this calcified. You really

THE PIRATE'S GUIDE TO SALES

got yourself a tough one."

Then, at last she spoke, but not to me. "Get that morcellator set up and show me how to use it. I can't justify waking this patient up to tell her we spent two hours and only got half of it."

I jumped into action and started giving instructions to the doctor and staff. Within minutes, she was working and using the new device like a pro and making good progress. Ten minutes then seemingly flew by and she finished up the procedure.

When the case ended, I said, "that was a tough case, but you've become so skilled in your methods that you made your first case with this look like you've done it for years."

She said, "well I'm sure it's gonna cost the OR and patient a lot of money, but I had no other choice."

And with that I knew the problem.

As it turned out Dr. R had been burned in the past. Having worked for a hospital and in private practice, she proceeded to open up about a story from her time in private practice where she was bamboozled by a rep that signed her up on a recurring contract that she couldn't break. Devices and orders kept coming in, despite the volumes of procedures requiring them slowing down. This of course was a burden on her cash flow and she could not get the device company to break the contract. She ended up losing lots of money and feeling as if she was misled and cheated. She went on to explain that to make matters worse, she saw on social media that the rep from the company that sold her the deal won a trip that year despite their shady approach. It was enough to jade her entire view of reps and turn her into what most reps now thought of as a "Scrooge" of a doc.

After listening to this story, I went on to explain a bit about myself and my upbringing and how I could completely understand her past experience leading to mistrust. I told her that from now on I could give her a price list for any items she might want to use, and she could compare them to the cost of her current items. My only request: that she take into account the cost per minute that is billed out in the OR and subtract time savings. She agreed this was fair and we ended up using our morcellators on 90 percent of her future cases. Had I not understood where she was coming from, I might have only gotten that one case or even worse gotten kicked out altogether.

When shifting perspective, avoid making assumptions at all cost. Try like hell to understand before being understood. Be patient and come into the situation with as much knowledge of where the other party is coming from as possible. Think in terms of the ghost of Christmas past, present, and future, and devise a path forward. View from the crow's nest (or at a safe distance at the back of the OR) and cast a vision of the future that you will bring to the table. Await your time and guide the customer to a new view!

CHAPTER
Twelve

GET WIND IN YOUR SAILS

Building Belief with Influence and Visualization

Okay, so we opened with empathy and honesty, then started shifting perspective like the sailing winds. Now it's time to build momentum with belief and influence and get those sails moving. This next part is what changes behavior, and that's the most challenging part of every sales encounter. Up to this point all you've wanted to achieve is to get the customer listening, asking questions, and beginning to trust that you may indeed have something of value. However, they likely still have a ton of doubt, and you're unlikely to move the needle any further without building belief, and making the perception a reality, until you bring it to life. In order to enact change, you have to cast a vision of what doing business with you long term will look like. Most are comfortable, or at least satisfied, with the situation they already have. Even if they aren't, disruption and change come with their own set of problems, so what you have to offer may simply look like another threat to the comfortable

94

status quo.

Let's look at two main ways to build belief and shift a customer's thinking towards an openness to real change: Influence and Visual Connection.

Part 1: Influence

Influence is created in three proven and sound ways. The first is with social norms. Think of social norms as the answer to "what is everyone else doing?" Social norms are the reason customer testimonials and celebrity spokespeople exist. The second way to create influence is loss aversion. Studies show we are far more loss averse than we are driven by gain. Show someone what they will lose if they don't make a change, and they are far more likely to do so. The third and final proven influencer we will discuss is the utilization of trusted sources. Think of trusted sources as stamps of validation that add weight to your words.

Social Norms

There was an episode of the show, *The Apprentice*, which perfectly highlighted the power of social norms. In the scene, entrepreneurs were given a street-side vending business to set up and run. They had 24 hours to come up with a plan, assemble a team, and launch their product. The goal was simple: the teams had one day to sell as much as they could, with the team that generated the most profit being the winner.

One of the teams, understanding what influences human behavior, had a brilliant idea. They paid a small group of people out of their marketing budget to stand in line and hang around their food truck. They were instructed to talk amongst themselves, eat, and look pleased with their meal. The outcome? While other nearby food trucks and vendors were struggling to get their first customers, the winning team had real paying customers flocking to see what everyone was crowded around for. If so many people had chosen their food truck, then to the various passersby, all these people milling around the food truck were social proof that what was being cooked up must be good. People even waited double and triple the time to get their food when other similar vendors had no line at all.

This little scenario isn't unique to one product or industry, either.

Social norms work for everything. Awhile back when I was learning the ropes of the medical device industry, I watched firsthand as the prior top rep at my company used social norms to perfection. Bryan Sackmann was a high energy diplomat with finely honed skills in the art of influence. On one particular occasion I specifically remember him saying, "We are going to stop in and get Dr. J to use this new device on his next case." I thought to myself, "well that's confident, and how on earth is he going to pull this off with no appointment or lunch?"

We stopped at the front desk of the doctor's office, and Bryan told the young woman at check-in that he was going back to see the surgery scheduler to check on cases. On the way back, he asked the nurse if Dr. J was with his last patient yet. As it turned out, Bryan had a schedule in his phone that showed all his top docs' calendars so he knew when he might be able to catch them without interrupting patient flow. He checked with the scheduler and found that Dr. J indeed had several procedures coming up in which he could benefit from using the new device. We then waited a bit and chatted it up with the scheduler, listening for the door to open from the patient room, indicating Dr. J was coming out of the room. When it did, Bryan popped out of his seat and said, "Dr J., I didn't want to drop in on you during patient hours, but I called to see how you were running and had hoped to catch you for a minute after your last patient to see if you are the right fit to be one of the first to trial our new device."

Bryan then said, "Dr. K, Dr. C, and Dr. P, have all put on cases, and I figured you wouldn't want to be left out."

Bryan's delivery almost sounded cheesy, and I remember wondering how Dr. J was going to react. His response: "Bryan, you son of a bitch, you know exactly what to say to get me to respond. If Dr. K, Dr. C, and Dr. P are going to be your first users, then I better get on the schedule with it or else no one is going to know how good or bad this device really works."

"What," I thought? He hasn't even seen the device, and he's loosely agreeing already? Then Bryan whipped the device out of his bag and began to tell Dr. J what got the other doctors interested. He then supported the claims of the benefits with a clinical study. Dr. J responded with a couple questions and then said, "I'm not sure if I have any cases coming up that I can use it on, but when I do, I'll give it a shot."

Bryan said, "I already checked with your scheduler and you have three coming up in the next month. I'll plan to be there. Will you let the scheduler know to switch the procedure and supply list for the hospital?" "You got it," said Dr. J, and we walked out with a new valuable user. Three new cases a month was $72,000 in revenue a year and the sale took less than two minutes to complete!

Two things caught my attention about the way Bryan approached selling. The first was that for a guy who on the surface seemed a bit scattered and disorganized, he prepared like crazy. He knew when he could see his docs without interfering with patient visits. He had a list of all the individual doctors' influencers, including who they went to school with, who they respected in the community, where they trained, etc. Then when the time came, he would have the peers and influencers sell to each other. He would keep a list of who was using what and where, and then say, "don't take it from me doc, which of your peers on this list would you want to check with to see how their experience has been thus far?"

The second thing about his approach that left an impact on me was his use of social norms for dinner programs. Instead of traditional dinner programs with one provider practices, he would host workshops and even vendor versus vendor debates. He often would even invite all the providers, staff, and influencers to one dinner program. Bryan was the king at creating traction with social interaction, and front in center to all this was peer influence. In this way, all he had to do was simply orchestrate and facilitate. Then he would set up shop, sit back, and watch his plan and peer influencers go to work for him.

Loss Aversion

As stated earlier, one of the thought leaders in the world of influence and persuasion is Robert Cialdini. In his book, *Influence – The Psychology of Persuasion,* he talks about the power of framing loss versus gain. They explain several real-world examples of this. In one example he explains an experiment where one group of participants was told about how much money they could gain every day through energy efficiency improvements. The other then was told how much they would lose if they continued doing nothing. The outcome? The group that had the loss framed had a 300 percent improvement in taking action! We are loss averse by nature, and nearly anything can be framed as an opportunity or sunk cost if appropriated correctly.

Years ago, while working with one of my counterparts in the field, I saw this in action. We were trying to get the group of doctors in agreement on doing hereditary cancer screening. In the past, nearly every rep I'd ever worked with would explain how many lives could be saved if the doctor was to identify all the mutation carriers for hereditary conditions such as BRCA 1 and 2. On this occasion, though, the rep took it upon himself to find out ahead of time how many patient charts the group themselves had. Then, instead of sharing the number of people they could potentially save, he shared how many mutation carriers still were undetected in their own population. Not only that, but he did so in a visual way. In this situation the doctors collectively saw 30,000 patients, of which roughly 210 patients statically were carriers with up to an 87 percent chance of cancer. These were 210 patients walking through their clinic each and every day that carried the absolute highest risk of getting cancer and the provider had no idea which ones they were. To add reality to this he took 210 Post-it notes shaped like women and added those to a huge four-by-six-foot Post-it board. His promise was that he would do everything in his power to help them systematically find and pull off one by one these 210 patients until they were all identified and protected from future cancer risk. For them to be able to see the sheer number of patients on one board, that carried such risk, then put the physicians in a different mindset entirely.

Trusted Sources

In some instances, you just don't have schools of social proof available. In others, maybe it's not needed at all to close the deal. You can usually still create belief with a few good, trusted sources supporting your cause. In a way similar to how Bryan used the list of doctors in his area as trusted sources, try hard to think of influencers that would pertain to your audience. If its medical sales often times this can come in the form of white papers, journal articles, and clinical studies. Outside the medical field it might come from the referencing of other trusted and legitimate companies that utilize your product or service. Lastly, if none of this exists yet, then it's time to create your own.

One of the most impactful ways to grow your business is organically. In the modern world we see this all the time with local bands. No doubt, what you consider a household name today, was nothing but a dive bar band years ago. How did they get out of the dive bar? They got influencers to like them. The local bars and clubs see potential, give them a chance, and slowly but surely the regulars at the bar start feeling an attachment. We all want to feel like we saw the next big act first and somehow live vicariously through their rise to stardom. Thus, those locals spread the word of the new hot act and news begins to spread regionally. The regional act then, still able to play the underdog card, and having more loyal fans, then empowers the new crop to spread their love. This continues slowly at first, but then perpetuates itself until it hits exponential growth that propels them to stardom.

However, it rarely if ever, was an overnight success, and most certainly it didn't happen without the nurturing of some early adopters and influencers. Sure, some big-name brands can pay Kylie Jenner and Selena Gomez half a million dollars for some posts to create some instant credibility; however, most success originates organically and starts small.

When you don't have trusted sources to pull from, create your own out of your early adopters. Every product and service has a select few who will try what you have. Find them, treat them overly well, ask for feedback, and make them part of the growth process. Your goal should be to create a select few brand groupies that will sell and influence for you. As the salesman or company owner, you can't be trusted, at least not in the beginning. You need to find, adopt, or create trusted sources to add credibility.

Find your influencers, use them, start small, and dream big. Then sit back and let others attempt to achieve your overnight successes!

Part 2: Using Visuals

Once you've identified what you will use in your call and sales funnel for influence, then it's time to make an emotional connection to it. This is where visuals come in. Part 2 of building belief and anchoring the sale is visual connection.

Visual Connection

The 2016 Grammy ballet for Album of the Year read like this ....
Adele{ ;) }, Justin Bieber { :O }, Drake { <_> }, and Sturgill
Simpson { #$@%*! }. Wait, who's Sturgill Simpson? At the time, he
was a little-known singer/songwriter from Kentucky on his third album's
studio release. Having spent a lifetime honing his craft already, Simpson
likely found himself both honored and shocked by this "nomination
from nowhere."

That, however, was beside the point because in the rote,
impressionistic, and predictable world of pop music just being on the
ballet was likely enough to put a lifetime stamp of validation on his work.
Simpson himself seemingly foreshadowed this juxtaposed reality in one
of his earliest songs when he wrote, "*a picture is worth a 1,000 words, but a
word ain't worth a dime. But they all know we'll go on talking til the end of time.*"

So, does this tried and true statement exist only because we are
uncomfortable with silence? Possibly. However, it's more likely we
spend less time on choosing our images as carefully as our words because
we don't see the value that's right in front of us. Think of all the
commercials comparing the old with the new, the celebrity with the
product, the familiar with the unfamiliar. Words by themselves pale in
comparison to what can be achieved in a singular moment of connection.
Experts tell us this is where the magic happens. If we want it
remembered, we better make that connection visual!

Link Influence with a Visual

Are you trying to teach a complicated subject matter to a brand-new
audience? What comparison can you draw to something they already
know? In the book, *Unlimited Memory,* author Kevin Horsley debunks the
myth of a photographic memory. The book teaches you exactly how
memory experts remember 1000s of data points, random lists, and
historical dates. How do they do it? You guessed it. You link the
unfamiliar with a visual map of something you already know.

To use an example, let's say you sell a product that offers only
marginally better results than the competition. For the sake of analogy
we might even put a number on that or a percentage. It's "1 percent
better" or "reduces time by 50 seconds." Is that going to resonate? What

if you go further and implore one of your influencers and extrapolate that number to show its compounding effects? Maybe if you use it 100 times that roughly 8.5 minutes or even 100 percent more output can be achieved. That's better, but it still doesn't provide staying power. It could be the customer doesn't appreciate doing math in their head or that their eyes gloss over when they hear numbers. Now, what if you add loss and a visual to your data? What would a picture that showed 100 percent more output look like? Or, for that matter, ever wonder why moments of silence have so much impact? It's certainly not the seconds that tick by. A moment of silence by yourself or with one other person is either a short cat nap with a narcolept or a creepy encounter. Add a stadium full of people and watch them all stop what they are doing and remain quiet for 30 seconds, and you've created a memory!

Make the Loss Visible

We already talked about the power of loss aversion, but the way to enhance it is with a visual. In a popular Ted Talk by Jeni Cross on behavior change, Jeni uses a basketball to explain heat loss in a home. She explains that the average home loses most of its energy around the seals of doors and windows. To frame up the lost energy, she explains that, even in efficient homes, windows lose "a basketball size" worth of air around worn seals. She then explains, "Imagine a kid throws a basketball through your window. Picture how much air is going through that hole and how much money is escaping every second it's not repaired. The reality is that hole exists in every home. It's just spread out, and as such, it's not nearly as visible."

Bring an Emotion to Life

What do horses and puppies have to do with beer? For Budweiser, they have meant home run after home run Superbowl commercial. Each year the top Superbowl commercials, based on ROI, almost always pull at viewers' heartstrings.

Try to think of ways to make a strong emotional connection to your product with an image or story. Be careful to make an actual connection, though, because for every story like Budweiser's connection to Clydesdales, there are ten just like it that failed. The easier it is for people

101

to see a connection the better.

Let's discuss some of the ways experts say to use visuals the right way!

Use the Data from Your Trusted Sources in a Visual Story

Data, metrics, and measurement have become king in baseball, business, fitness, and in just about every facet of life. We are flooded with data points that often mean nothing to us personally. However, remember what Peter Drucker famously said? "If you can't measure it, you can't improve." So, with data so important in our lives, how do we win with so much of it? You guessed it; tell a story.

A famous example of this was Google in 2016. Google is the king of data, and with a tie to every person in the world, how do you make individual interest relevant in a sea of search? The answer was right in front of them. They took the top searches of the year and made an emotional "state of the nation" year in review video. The ad was the most successfully measured ROI of 700 technology ads tested that year!

Make Your Message Be Remembered

Hear a piece of information and three days later you will remember ten percent of it. Add a picture and you will remember 65 percent. Our memory is strongly tied to visuals. Without good pictures you can bet 90 percent of what you just said will be forgotten by week's end. Knowing this, how much information from this past week did you share that has now been forgotten?

When distraction is needed

In a famous experiment done by Harvard University dubbed "The Invisible Gorilla," participants were asked to count the number of passes a ball made between six people wearing black and white shirts. In the middle of the video a man in a gorilla suit strolls right through the scene. When asked if the participants noticed the man in the gorilla suit, only 50 percent did. The experiment revealed just how much information we miss that's right in front of us when our focus is placed elsewhere.

Putting It All Together

Okay, we covered a lot here, but as stated earlier, belief and influence are what creates behavioral change and what will ultimately drive impact. Therefore, let's briefly recap the goals and tactics.

When you think of influence, remind yourself that rarely do we put any thought into what has or hasn't worked to change our own habits. Ultimately those "in your face" tactics that come to mind when you hear the word "influence" likely didn't resonate. However, think of times you did find yourself changing your views or behaviors. What prompted it? Chances are you will find that social norms, trusted sources, and/or the fear of loss were behind it. What worked for Bryan and so many bands out there works across industry, product, and genre. Find your influencers and use them.

Then, once you have your influencers, plan to present and speak to them with visual connection. Be reminded that without a visual connection to your most important messaging, that 90 percent of what you've spent so much time planning to present will be forgotten within three days. Find the key elements you need to get across and make and emotional connection with something that the customer already can relate too. Building belief and momentum in the sale is the key to behavior change. Find what works for you and your territory and get wind in your sails!

CHAPTER
Thirteen

FOLLOW THE CURRENT

V.A.L.U.E and Solutions Tied to Why

It was the national sales meeting of a prominent medical device company, and Ryan was anxious. He knew he had a chance to win rep of the year, and as such, a speech would be required. Having finished in the top ten percent of the sales ranks six other times, Ryan was no stranger to winning the prestigious President's Club award and had knocked on the door a couple years in a row for the top salesperson in the company.

All that he could handle. The possible speech, though, was another story. To Ryan selling wasn't about winning awards or speeches, it was about bringing value to his customers. If Bryan's secret sauce to winning was influence and social norms, then Ryan's was having his customers see him as a valuable asset to their team. Delivering a speech was certainly something he could confidently and comfortably do, but it was never his goal. His focus had always been delivering value and continually finding ways to reinvent himself and his products.

Having known Ryan Zimmer for years, I couldn't think of a better person to interview and analyze for the value stream portion of the sales approach. When I called him and asked him what had made him so successful over the years, his reply was, "my goal is to have the customer not even think they are being sold anything."

He went on to explain, "when I leave a sales call, I want the customer saying, 'well that was helpful, insightful, productive, etc.' I want them thinking I'm different than most salespeople because I come prepared with value-driven solutions. In that manner, when you set up a give and take, consultative approach, the customer learns to trust and respect what you bring." You see, to Ryan, selling isn't about what can be seen or said, it's about what you bring. The cheapest product is no good if it has to be replaced or never worked in the first place. In a similar sense the most expensive or luxurious products aren't of much value if it's difficult to use or get support for. Value comes in many different forms and can even be created. What you bring, in conjunction with your product, is how you maximize value.

So, all speeches aside (and yes he won and delivered a beautiful speech), let's look at some ways to create value!

Goal of Value Proposition – Future State Tied to Why

What something is worth is dependent on the value seen in the eyes of the receiver. Following the current then is akin to mapping a value stream that ties to the most essential needs of the customer. In order to do so properly we need to anchor our value directly to the customer's motivations. Try selling the features of an engine in a BMW to a guy who only wants it for status. Now, my friend, you've exited the current. On the contrary, tell him you just sold the same model to Lebron James' cousin, and that it's the last one, and you've found flow. Value can come in many different forms and from various parts of the customer's business, but there is always a flow. Understanding where you can impact and provide help along that flow of goods or services will enhance the consultative approach to selling a solution.

There are two steps to understanding a customer's value chain. The first, the anchor, was explained in chapter six, where we covered how to observe and map a customer's current state. How does the customer currently get from A to B, and where are the sticking points that seem to cause an issue or opportunity? After analyzing the customer's current state, you can cut the fat and begin to formalize a vision for what the future might look like.

In step two, which is the part of the sale itself, you'll propose a solution that casts a vision of what business with you will look like in the future. How will business with you improve, reduce, increase, or eliminate inconsistencies? Or, to consider our earlier Scrooge metaphor, how can you be the ghost of Christmas to come, delivering presents under the tree that the customer never realized he or she even needed?

In general, there are five areas where this value can be identified. To keep it simple, we'll use the acronym of V.A.L.U.E. to define them.

V. Variability

Variability is the first area of potential value we'll evaluate. Much like the definition of the word itself, it can come in many different forms. Does the customer experience inconsistency in product or service? Do they experience inconsistent or unpredictable outcomes? Is there misalignment within the organization of the most important goals? Do their processes vary? In all of these instances, if variability exists there's opportunity for value. Can you increase the chances of reliability? If so, ask yourself if the audience you're presenting to cares. If they do, then chances are this should be part of your solution and value proposition.

A. Automation

How many sales presentations come off self-serving? Honestly? Somewhere between a lot and most. Being a consultant to your customer is a way to separate yourself, and automation is an area almost all customers need help in. How can you help to streamline information, processes, follow-up, data collection, and even reduce human error? In the modern world of technology and its integration, understanding how to help your customers on that front will help regardless of the industry. Can you assist them in tracking orders or shipments? Can you help them integrate patient data into EMR? Can you improve customer satisfaction with engagement and follow-up?

Many of you might be saying to yourself, "technology and automation have nothing to do with what I sell." Let's use a couple examples to illustrate just how mistaken you might be. In my first sales gig I sold ocean and air freight forwarding services for UPS. While UPS is one of two kings in the package delivery business, at the time they were a small fish in the freight-forwarding world. There were, and still are, hundreds of competitors in this space because the barrier to entry in freight forwarding is low. Similar to the logistics of trucking industries, all you really needed back then was a phone and a sales' force to book shared space on other companies' planes and ships. When there's a lot of competition, price becomes the obvious and first negotiation point. Being a smaller player at the time, UPS didn't have the purchasing power to be the lowest cost carrier. So how did we win business? You guessed it, with technology and automation. What UPS did have from its sophisticated packaging business was technology. We found customers who had time sensitive goods and needed to know where their shipment was at all times, when it would arrive, and how or if it was held up in customs at the ports of entry. By giving the customer sophisticated tracking at the click of a button, and by helping them reduce man hours needed to get shipments through customs, we could win business at a higher cost. Every encounter with a new customer would start with cost as the dominant concern. By the end, cost became an afterthought. Once we were able to show customers how much money we could save them automating the shipping process, the difference in cost became a non-issue. By finding and quantifying opportunity costs you can win in highly competitive industries where you may be a higher-priced option.

L. Lower Cost

There are a number of other places you can look to lower costs as well. What are the short-term and long-term costs associated with how a customer currently does business? Can you show them a long-term savings that outweighs a short-term sunk cost? Can you improve cash flow or reduce interest expenses to offset a higher price?

Oftentimes, we get tunnel vision when we look at the cost associated with what's in front of us. However, by shifting perspective and looking at both the associated long-term and short-term costs, it's often easy to balance the playing field.

There are a few products in my own life that I have learned to spend extra money on upfront because the longevity far outweighs the cost associated with repeat purchases. For instance, I never buy cheap furniture. For the most part, if you get a traditional looking piece of furniture, built right, it won't go out of style and will last far longer. We used to have to buy new couches every few years because the pillows would sag, and the frame would wear down. Buying a good quality couch that costs a third more is easily justifiable if it lasts two or three times longer.

Paint a picture of cost that correlates with the whole picture. Car salespeople do the opposite of this when negotiating on monthly payment instead of the total cost of the vehicle. While this book isn't meant for the one-time purchase, one could argue even a car salesperson needs to build trust to get repeat purchases down the road. Instead of skewing the numbers like a car salesperson, be a consultant and do an honest vision cast of all costs associated and compare and contrast apples to apples.

U. Uniquely Differentiate

In order for your customers to create sustainability, they need to have a unique offering and a way to fend off competition. The unique offering is the special sauce and their defense of competition is the moat that surrounds the castle. Any time you can aid your customers in either area you'll increase their profitability. A competitive advantage almost always equates to increased profits, so if you can help customers uniquely separate themselves or protect from other companies or businesses in the industry, your message (and services) will likely be heard.

E. Excess Waste

Waste comes in many forms and exists in every organization. Does the customer know the time wasted on duplicated processes? Are they unknowingly passing increased costs to patients or customers? Do they waste material or money because of loose ends?

Anywhere there's waste there's an opportunity to generate more profitability and increased efficiency. Knowing your audience and your customer is crucial, but you can set yourself apart by including waste reduction in your value proposition.

In order to find waste, you almost always need to "go to the gemba" and see for yourself how a customer operates. Customers themselves become blind to waste, so it's not always apparent. They may have even written it off as unfixable. Follow the flow and distribution of their patterns and look for areas that create a bottleneck. Remember the toothpaste factory story from chapter six? In that example, had upper management gone to the gemba and followed the flow they would have realized a $20 solution before implementing a $12 million one. Ask a lot of questions and do your research. Then deliver waste reduction as part of your solution.

Putting It All Together

When you think of value, think of what won Ryan so many president's clubs. Every other rep in that company had the same products, training, and much of the same skill set. The difference was that Ryan was able to add value to each and every product and interaction. How can you be a consultant to your customers? In what areas can you guide them or enhance their business or product that others can't or haven't thought of? Create value and define a future state of what business with you will look like. By doing so, you'll win every time.

In addition, much like every part of the six points of sail/sale, you have to ask yourself if the value you are providing anchors to the customer's why. Map out your solution, including all the elements of V.A.L.U.E. you think you can bring. Then ask yourself if the customer cares about each element. Reduce the list to the items that tie to the why. Only include things that don't make that connection if you're confident you can create a new perspective with the addition. Less is always more when you're doing the talking. The goal of your value proposition and this chapter is not to present on all the areas of potential value, but only the ones that are going to matter. The goal of the next chapter and the negotiation is not to win on everything. Instead what you ultimately want to do is guide the sale to winning on the 20 percent non-negotiables and leave the other 80 percent as items you can give away to have the customer feel like they've won.

CHAPTER

Fourteen

WALK THE PLANK

Tactile Negotiation to Guide you to Close

In 2000, Reed Hastings offered to sell his online DVD rental company to Blockbuster for a mere $50 million dollars. Ignoring all the intangible market signs, then-Blockbuster CEO John Antioco quickly ended negotiation talks with his "new competitor," citing that the niche product was losing money.

"No Deal," Antioco said, without considering the opportunity that was ultimately addressing the future of his business and consumer behavior. Today, Netflix is valued at more than *$50 billion*, and the neighborhood Blockbuster stores, once bustling with life, are now home to parking lots and ice cream parlors.

So what's the psychology behind bad negotiations? What hardwired human behaviors cause us to give up far more than we need to or should? Or, as with the case of Antioco, what causes us to completely ignore the intangibles and make short-sighted choices? Can we learn to be better negotiators, or are some of us just better at it than others? In his book *Never Split the Difference*, Chris Voss writes, "Without a deep understanding of human psychology... the acceptance that we are all crazy, irrational, impulsive, emotionally driven animals...all the raw intelligence and mathematical logic in the world is little help in the fraught shifting interplay of two people negotiating."

In reading two recent books from ex-FBI hostage negotiators, the secret to a successful negotiation seems to stem from a better understanding of human behavior. The goal of negotiation is not to win but to have the other party feel like they won without giving up what you need. To again apply the Pareto rule, you want to decide ahead of time on the most important 20 percent achievable(s) that you're unwilling to bend on. Use and sacrifice the remaining 80 percent as bargaining chips. The trick is to do this strategically. Find items in that 80 percent that you would like to have and that you know the customer will in fact require. Then spend some time on these negotiables, instead of opting to immediately show that you are indeed willing to sacrifice them. The goal of tactile negotiation is to anchor the giveaways on the customer's why so that they feel they have a choice and some control in the manner.

Let's discuss five pirate tips that will help you navigate walking the plank.

Tips that come from Voss's *Never Split the Difference*, and *What Every BODY is Saying* by Joe Navarro.

Tactile Empathy

Forget about winning. *To repeat: the goal should be to have the other side feel like they won.* To achieve this you better start with some open-ended questions—listen, pay attention, and use tactile empathy. The technique requires flexibility and an understanding of the other party's perspective in the moment. Body language experts such as Joe Navarro tell us that the owners of even the greatest poker faces have "tells" elsewhere on their body. Pay attention to sudden changes in movement. Try to decode whether the other party is feeling threatened, vulnerable, excited, nervous, or irritated. Then adjust to that information, changing your tactics and questioning approaches to show empathy to their situation.

111

The Black Swan

Every negotiation includes intangibles that, in hindsight, had tremendous influence on the outcome. Take the Netflix/Blockbuster deal for instance. While none of us were at the table, it would be reasonable to believe that ego, vulnerability, and mutual trust played a role in the failure to strike a deal. While we now know John Antioco hurt his company by not making a deal, Netflix was likely just as culpable in this negotiation. It's easy to say now that Netflix made the right call, but at the time they were losing money hand over foot as a mail order and return service. The streaming platforms that we see today weren't monetized in any business modeling done at that time. So, it's conceivable to believe, that even for Netflix luck played its part. Had a few things not gone their way and/or had they refused to change with the market, Netflix too could have run out of money before reaching success.

In *Never Split the Difference,* Voss suggests we try to uncover the "Nos" as early and often as we can in the negotiation with a goal of getting the other party to say "that's right." Your goal should be to "bend the other party's reality" and guide them to "making the decision you want them to make." "That's right" is a sign of negotiation progress.

Mirror and Label

Mirror means repeating back the key last part of the person's phrase in the form of a question. The trick here is to show you heard what they said, acknowledge it, and want them to explain further. You are "labeling" what they are saying to make sure it's important to them, but you're also trying to get them to divulge more specifics. Chris Voss recommends pausing at least four seconds to let the person talk more. Use a calm, even-toned voice, and try to get the other person to give up as many specifics as you can.

Be Specific

Specifics are the keys to a negotiation, but you want to reveal yours second. The more specific figures, details, personality traits, likes and dislikes you can learn about the other party, the more likely you will be to successfully reach an endpoint.

Imagine the psychological impact you could have next time you counteroffer on a house just with the specific price of $294,500. Let's say originally you offer $275,000, they counter at $315,000, and you final at $294,500. With no other details at all, the other party is likely to think, "Wow, they have a specific reason they aren't willing to go any higher." Specific details give insight into other people's thoughts. The more you are spending time on their position, the less likely they are to know how high or low you were willing to go before all this started.

Understand the Goal

Remember the goal? It isn't to win, but to have them think they won. Abe Lincoln's famous quote still rings true today: "A drop of honey catches more flies than a gallon of gall." Don't go into a negotiation with the mindset of getting what you want. Instead lead with a mindset of discovery and seek to find out their bottom line. The more they are talking and in agreement the better the negotiation is likely going. Always remember you can win an argument but lose on the negotiation. Ideally you want to create a mutually beneficial agreement.

Putting It All Together

Now that you understand the goal and some tactics to get you there, it's time to again anchor your negotiation to the why. In hindsight, it's pretty easy to see why John Antioco and Blockbuster should have taken the Netflix deal. Considering that didn't happen, we can assume something was missing from this negotiation. What was it that John Antioco needed to hear to keep negotiation talks alive? Could it have been that pride and internal struggles for power kept these two from a mutually beneficial deal?

Find the why and understand the motive to buy. Reframe all the items up for bid at the end, and then restate what you have conceded to allow the deal to move forward. Tie each item to their need and remind the other party of how they struck the deal for every one of them. Then begin to frame up the path forward by highlighting the work you are about to do for them and get ready to deliver the gold!

CHAPTER
Fifteen

DELIVER THE GOLD

Closing with S.M.A.R.T Asks

With seven Presidents' Club wins and four account manager of the year awards, Rocky Baker's sales career is the stuff of legends. However, like most things in life, the success that created the wins didn't come from the most obvious of experiences. "The best sale of my career was nowhere near the most lucrative," said Rocky. "In fact, I barely made any money on the deal. But here I am, ten years later, still reaping the benefits of a lesson learned and a career in sales."

For Rocky, what comes so naturally now wasn't always so easy. Like many, his unique selling style and brand developed over time and with experience. Looking back, it's easy to see the progression from good to great, but in hindsight this is always the case, right? So how did he get there and what were the keys?

Prior to this particular sales encounter and like most before him, Rocky used to be successful by being a product expert and mainly selling on features and benefits. However, as he stated, "I'll never forget the comment that hit me like a ton of bricks and changed my views of selling forever." He went on to explain, "I still remember vividly the faces and words spoken so bluntly and true. Their comments to me were, 'why should we go through all the trouble for something that is only marginally more efficacious for our patients?' And, just like that the light bulb went off."

Rocky was sure others had felt this way and likely even said something similar, but he didn't have a work around and thus had ignored it. But, he thought, how many sales had he lost right at the end simply because he hadn't provided enough value to justify a big change for a small benefit?

Truly wanting to avoid this situation, Rocky decided to push for more information. He thanked the customer for their candid feedback and asked if he could learn more about their business. How were they incentivized? In addition, aside from the obvious patient outcomes what was most important to the practice, to the provider, to the institution as a whole?

To his surprise, the client gave him very honest and straightforward answers, and from this point on Rocky tried to differentiate himself and his product. "Looking back the switch in my approach was to look at the business through the lens of value-based medicine. While they didn't call it that then, the concept was the same. The goal, more often than not, was to provide the best outcomes, at the lowest cost to the patient and system, and do it with the least amount of hassle and disruption to flow as possible."

Rocky distinctly remembers going back in, shortly after re-pitching his value proposition and doing research, and tying his product solutions to their needs. "It was amazing to me that with the same product, and the same person delivering it, I could get a yes when I walked in with a real solution tied to all their objections and needs."

From that point on Rocky prepared differently for his interactions with his doctors. He found out ahead of time what they needed, wanted, and had to have in order to move forward. Then he delivered a value proposition tied to every one of them. In this way he had so much confidence going into the close that it was more of a "tell" than an ask.

"By the time I get to closing, I know they are in our camp and they know I'm in theirs," he said. "In that way they want someone with a plan. Someone who will come in and take action and leave as few steps and action items to them as possible. It's the difference between a "hopeful" ask and a confident "tell or instruction.""

The New Close

As stated at the onset of *The Points of Sail,* and as described by Rocky's success, closing is much different than the scenes depicting it in movies. It's not nearly as confrontational or conniving, and as such should be far less scary than most make it out to be. Still, many don't do it correctly, and a good number don't do it at all. I suspect part of the reason most are uncomfortable with closing is because they haven't really shown any value that would warrant asking for anything in return. Asking for something with absolutely no idea whether the customer needs or wants it, just leads to uncertainty, fear, and doubt. Considering this, it's no wonder that asking for things can at times seem fast-laned for rejection.

Let's change that forever. Right now. You have done your research and have delivered a unique value proposition to the customer. Therefore, you have earned the right to ask and close. You clearly have something of value that you're bringing to the show. Don't for one second allow fear to creep in. Much like Rocky's story with closing, you have to know they will say yes and layout the plan for them. You are driving this ship and helping guide the customer now, not the other way around. Deliver the Gold with confidence and watch as they willingly accept it!

Still, that's perhaps easier said than done. So, in the name of getting you to an honest and successful close, let's look at five S.M.A.R.T asks to include.

Specific

Through your planning and negotiation, you've settled on the 20 percent deliverables you expect. Specifically state what these expectations are and check in with the customer to make sure they understand them. Here is where specifics need to be clearly defined. Do you need a contract signed? Do you need a time commitment from them? Do you need purchase of something today in order to justify the continued relationship? None of this should be sprung on the customer. You were leading towards this point from the negotiation, and now you're just stating it with specifics.

Measurable

Once you have specifically stated the requirements, begin to formulate how you will track progress and milestones. Alignment should have taken place with the customer's goals so make measurements around this. What are the goals and how will you know progress is being made towards them? Let's revisit the personal trainer analogy from chapter four: they have hired you as their personal trainer to fix a problem, improve an outcome, or change their current business practices. How can either of you know you are achieving what was expected without measurement? Find the measurements that will be key indicators of success. Map out to the best of your abilities what good looks like and set goals for each key metric of success.

Assignable

Who will be responsible for what and what are the expectations of those responsibilities? If the customer is asking you to do all the work and has no role themselves, then you're setting yourself up for a quick exit. You can't show your kids how to do something without having them learn themselves, just as you can't do it all for your customers. They need to invest in the process as well. After all, you've become partners in this endeavor. As such, they have to do their part. Assign tasks that align with the goals and ask for their involvement.

Realistic

Here is where you need to do some expectation setting. Some things never go as planned, and as the customer's consultant you have insight on where these trouble spots typically show.

Set expected outcomes, a bottom line, and a stretch goal for each of the key performance and result indicators. If you are in the medical business, you should be very familiar with this process. Usually the key performance indicators are going to center around patients, which means the doctor themselves have another party involved in order to hit the goals. Patients in need of medicine, surgery, or testing vary, so at times the numbers will fluctuate. If you and your customer aren't hitting numbers initially, it may catch up later. That's okay as long as you are both seeing continuous improvement. Explain what you'd expect them to see and use the patient volumes as the denominator. By doing so you can then use percentages for goal tracking, instead of total patient volume, which inherently fluctuates.

Time Bound

The last checkpoint for a good ask is the addition of a timeframe. Often, asking for something in the future without a time limit is going to lead to simply "kicking the can down the road." It's human nature to put things off until tomorrow, so the more time constraints you can get agreement on the better. Check in with the customer to see what timeline is acceptable, and then make sure they are willing to instruct all members of their internal team to hit these dates and times as well.

Putting It All Together

When framing up your asks in the close, make sure you align and tie the key performance indicators and achievable(s) to the customer's why. Think like Rocky and try to deliver on value. Then close in a confident, captain-like manner.

The preparation you've put in and the consultative work you're about to do has gotten you this far. On every item on which you can align, restate the goal and plan it out all the way to the end. Check and double check that you're meeting the customer's expectations and that they are willing to meet your expectations as well. By doing so you can confidently close and prepare for a future partnership that will grow and sustain in the days, weeks, months, and even years to come!

CHAPTER

Sixteen

PLOTTING THE COURSE

Metrics and Sustainability

Ever close some highly sought-after business only to get a sinking feeling that you won't be able to pull it through? Often this happens with the largest of wins. There's good reason for this feeling. Consider that contracts can be broken, items can be returned, and promises can go unfilled. Just getting a commitment or contract for business doesn't mean you will keep it. It's up to you or your company to live up to your promise as much as it's up to the customer to live up to theirs.

Once you've closed the sale, the trick becomes keeping the business and growing it. The best way to achieve this is through setting up key performance indicators and imploring the PDCA method discussed

119

earlier. In order to manage, achieve, and control the desired results you're looking for, you must measure the right things and plan incrementally. Plot your path forward, and plan strategically through vision and experimentation.

KPIs

Let's start with key performance indicators (KPIs). This term is thrown around a lot in business today, but rarely do we see it utilized to its fullest potential. There's a difference between collecting raw data and calling it metrics, and strategic measurement with an aim for progress. What, how, and when you collect data and present it is far more important. It guides a path forward that sets expectations and allows for areas of improvement.

There are three key steps to analyzing and setting up KPIs: raw data collection, progress, and change. However, while most will start with collecting raw data, hope to make progress, and then make changes when it doesn't come to fruition, the true resolve comes from reversing the order.

Still not understanding what this has to do with selling or with your industry? Allow me to make an example out of myself from my first sales job selling ocean and air freight services. There are times in your career where you look back to where you started and realize why things didn't work out. Like many, a lot of key learnings happened from the early failures in my first job selling. I specifically remember selling a huge contract for Wayne Water Pumps to handle all their import business. It was a contract worth nearly a million dollars a year in business. I sold the business with a promise to improve on shipping time, reduce customs hold times at the ports of entry, and by adding visibility to their shipment tracking.

What I failed to explain, out of fear perhaps, was that any time you switch freight-forwarding services this get messy for a bit. When you change who's doing your customs brokerage, it's typical for the first few shipments to get held up. In addition, until the new customs' broker has all the material assigned with correct documentation, there's often more required back and forth in the beginning of the relationship than with the current or prior freight broker.

So, what happened? You guessed it: because I didn't set proper expectations, the first few shipments nearly became our last. They experienced hold times that caused the shipments to take even longer than they had with their current carrier.

Even worse, they experienced damaged goods because of improper crating. While the crating turned out to be the factory's fault, the delays and extra phone calls weren't exactly what the customer hoped for. I did my best to smooth things over and fix the damage done, but I'm still not sure we ever got remotely close to getting all the business promised.

Let's look back and break down what happened in an effort to highlight the importance of setting upfront expectations and KPIs. The customer, trusting me and my word thought it made sense to give us some early test shipments with product and ports of entry they were already experiencing challenges on. The thinking: if we could do what we said, then we could at least help them in this area now, thus proving our worth. However, all I saw was the early win and failed to explain that we would want to get some easier shipments first. We would need time to get our customs brokers up to snuff with all the product codes and paperwork needed to clear customs. All I would have needed to do to avoid this situation would have been to explain and plot the path forward, setting parameters on what good would look like.

Using this example, let's reverse time and the order of how key performance indicators are usually done. Instead of starting with the raw data collection, then measuring progress and making change, imagine if I had started with the change first. If I sold correctly then I would have set some expectations in the close and gotten a firm commitment. Then starting with what changes would occur and framing the expectations wouldn't have been as big of a deal.

Strong key performance indicators should be chosen with the goal of change. In addition, the progress should be set up to happen incrementally, not overnight. Lastly, you need to understand how the data will be collected, aggregated, and disseminated. In doing things this way, you've reversed the order, saved yourself a lot of time, and clearly defined the performance measures that matter. In essence you're doing exactly what we did on the sale itself and starting with the why.

Let's break down the three parts of setting Key Performance Indicators.

Incremental Change

Understand up front what changes will need to happen for you and the customer to be happy and set expectations for each other. This is a partnership, and you are the trusted advisor. Your customer will understand and appreciate you being upfront with the change that will occur. Furthermore, this ensures they won't be caught off guard (remember my failing?) when that change happens. If you're selling a device, then this might be setting expectations on training, early case outcomes, and your time availability. If you're selling equipment, it might be on the maintenance and retooling. Whatever the industry, if your customer is buying from someone new, there will be something different; therefore, the customer needs to understand what happens next. Tell them, and even have them repeat it back to you. Then set your key performance measurements around that.

Progress

Progress should be done incrementally. You don't want to change things all at once or overnight, but instead implore what the lean six sigma culture calls Kaizen. Kaizen is a Japanese term that means "continuous change" or "continuous improvement". Set a benchmark for where you want to start and cast a vision on where you and the customer want to end up. Once you have identified the areas needing changes and have plotted the path for how you will get there, progress becomes the map for less disruptive and more sustainable success.

Raw Data Collection

Now this last part becomes easy. Imagine starting with mountains of raw data with no idea what to pull out of it or how to benchmark it. This is precisely why it should come last. You have set both the goals for you and your customer, you've identified the path to getting there, and now the raw data jumps right off the page and you can mine it for gold. Set benchmarks from your early data so that you can use it to track progress and create change. Novel, huh?

PDCA

So that's the measurement part. Now for the sustainable part. There's a method to creating change and sustainability that's as old as time. It's called the scientific method, but in business and in lean philosophy, which we've discussed a lot, it's called the Plan, Do, Check, Act method.

While it's as simple as it sounds, it does take some obvious work. Create a plan or early test, implore it, check the outcomes to your KPIs, and take action to make corrections where needed. It's the "fail fast but don't fall too far model." Remember that sustainability happens with incremental change and at the speed with which you and the customer can handle it.

Putting It All Together

So that's it. Close with confidence and then the real work begins. Metrics and measurement will become your path forward. Formulate a few key performance indicators tied to the most-valued needs of the client, set proper expectations for attainment, plot the progress, make adjustments, and incrementally grow from within.

A properly planned and executed customer pull through can create a future trusted source. Target your best clients to be your future sales asset. Building solid case studies as examples only helps your business expand and scale that much faster. As Leonardo Da Vinci famously wrote, "Plot your course to a star, and you can navigate any storm."

C ONCLUSION

BURN THE BOATS!!!

Recap the Voyage

On May 6, 2019, my dad suddenly passed away. Having just celebrated his 60th birthday the Friday before with family and friends, the news of his death hit all of us hard.

In the weeks to follow, I continued to try to make sense of life and my purpose. In some ways this had less to do with his passing and was instead more of an inner soul searching. For years I had feared such a thing happening because of his deteriorating health. Nothing, however, could have prepared me for the real thing.

Two weeks after his death, and having gone back to my daily routine, I found myself questioning everything. Why couldn't he get help for his alcoholism? Why would he choose to live in such a miserable existence with so much potential?

As I sat in a hotel restaurant pondering such things on a trip to Parkersburg, West Virginia, an elderly man approached and pulled up a seat next to me. Looking disheveled, and peering over at me with sad, beady eyes, he asked me if I had stayed here before. I replied "no" and proceeded to stare down at the menu in front of me like a jerk.

Ten minutes later he showed yet another attempt to strike up a friendly conversation with a stranger. He asked me if I was a fan of the show "Game of Thrones." I still had no interest in chatting, and I stubbornly replied "no" and continued to stare down at my menu.

Then something came over me. Somewhere, a part of me felt I shouldn't dismiss his attempts at conversation. I told him I hadn't been watching TV lately but had heard so much about the show. "What is it you like about the show," I asked? He explained that every episode from the beginning to end expanded on the next and left him wanting to know how it would end. He couldn't remember a time he had ever been so emotionally attached to a show.

After several back-and-forth questions on the popular TV series, one thing led to another and the conversation started to expand towards real life. Two hours seemingly flew by. Dr. Bob, as it turned out, was a retired dentist from the DC area and had never had kids. He had always wanted to, but it just wasn't in his cards. He and his wife had been married for years, and she had recently passed. We shared stories of life, death, pain, love, and friendship.

I rarely, if ever, enter conversations about such topics with a stranger, but something about this guy's kind heart and openness made me feel comfortable. It quickly became clear to me that Dr. Bob had a unique ability to connect with people. In some regards I must have done the same for him because as dinner wrapped up and I said my goodbyes, Dr. Bob looked to me and sincerely said, "I greatly appreciated our conversation, and I'll never forget it."

I shared a similar sentiment, and we actually hugged each other prior to departing. I'm not even good at hugging my loved ones, and here I was hugging a stranger!

As I exited the restaurant, something occurred to me. This is what my dad had done his whole life. He embraced vulnerability, wore humility as a badge of honor, and genuinely listened to others. My guess is that my dad had countless Dr. Bob's in his life. Yet, there I was, 34 years of life behind me, and finally meeting my first one! While it was a simple exchange of words, I realized Dr. Bob's words were true, and his lesson to me paramount. I would never forget that conversation, and I never wanted to go back to fake, surface, conversations with strangers again.

In a similar way, this book culminates my career journey so far with an attempt at a conversion, or an awakening, of sorts. I've shared some key learnings and turning points I've encountered and perhaps you will soon as well. Like my encounter with Dr. Bob, these were all simple points in time where something was learned, and from which there would never be a return to the old way. There's an old story of the ancient explorer Hernan Cortes that is perfectly analogous to this commitment to the future.

Legend has it that Cortes captained his crew across stretches of rough ocean waters. The journey was long, and his men were tired. Upon arriving, he did the unthinkable. He instructed his men to burn the boats they came in on. His men must have been perplexed and scared by the proposition; however, as Cortes explained, "there was no going back." Success in the new world was the only option, and the ships that had guided them there would now only serve symbolically as weakness. What had gotten them to a new and better place must now be left behind and the knowledge gained used for future voyages.

As this book now comes to a close and ends its own destination, we hope you remember the journey. Where have you gone and where do you want to go? Remember the tools and strategies that got you where you are today. Pirate what you like about this book and make it your own. And please, please, please keep searching for new and better ideas to steal and share. We can all achieve so much more if we learn to pirate the open seas ahead!

QUICK RECAP ON THE VOYAGE NOW TAKEN

Part 1: The Prep

Now that we have plotted the path of the customer, it's time to take a look back over the path and course we took here.

If you remember from the beginning of this book, the mind map correlates with the ship and voyage. In part one, preparing for the voyage, we discussed the eight parts of the ship that correlate to skill sets and concepts in selling. We started with the destination and picked our stretch and S.M.A.R.T. goals, and then worked our way back. In real life, and in sales, this is where we want to start as well. Begin by envisioning where you want to land, and then use specific, measurable, assignable, realistic, and time bound goals to get you there.

The next thing we did was give a name to the vessel that was to lead us to our destination. Self-analysis is important in understanding where you're coming from, where you are now, and what's most important in the future. Just as the most powerful brands in the world stand for something, we too need to let our strengths and attributes shine through. Rarely do you ever see a powerful brand that you can't describe in three words. Find your unique offering and start to embody it, wearing it on your sleeve and in your heart.

Then outfit your boat and use the bulkhead storage in an effort and manner in which someone who has conquered ADHD would. View the daily struggles as a gift. Use them to your advantage and avoid anything that looks remotely like a curse. Adjust your morning to start off on the right foot and deal with downtime in a productive way.

Remember how the H in ADHD stands for helping stay the course? Use your resources and technology like navigation tools, instead of distractions. Pick one ecosystem for calendaring, emailing, and data analysis, and tie them all together. Turn off the notifications on your email and phone when you aren't in dedicated periods of time for batching that kind of work.

We also discussed disruptive habits. Stop the negative self-talk and put all your self-defeat in a box. While you can't completely avoid having these things—we all do to some degree—just know how to put them out of your mind, and captain your vessel unburdened. When you're really down, call a friend or do something more positive before allowing things to snowball.

In chapter five we assembled our crew and took ownership of our role as captains. We learned lessons of human behavior from some of the brightest minds of past and present. We also got advice on how to influence those around you and assemble a team of ground troops who will help keep you on track and lighten the load. Let your crew eat first and treat others in a way that's akin to how you would treat someone you're responsible for, like a friend or family member.

In chapter six we pulled anchor and learned about finding the why. Just as Simon Sinek so poetically explained in his golden circle video, start with the why. After, everything else falls into place. Through his methods, Wim Hof has been a huge influence on my life, and on the lives of many others, but if he hadn't found his own why, no one would have heard of him. Getting others to see the impact that being happy, healthy, and strong had on his own life led his method practitioners to him.

In chapters seven, eight, and nine we learned how to plan with a map, prospect with a compass, and target with a cannonball. Planning requires routing, funneling, and scheduling around your core meetings that are essential staples on your calendar. Prospecting requires understanding who and when, at times that don't know where. Much like Laird Hamilton's approach to surfing, you have to know which waves to take on and how to embrace crashes and misses. The cannonball strategy will help you find what is needed to be patient and focused.

The last chapter of part one was on decision making using both your systems. When there was no wind, the pirates used oars. It was slower, but it got the job done. The wind was fast but could lead them off course, and in stormy weather they were forced to take the sails down. Without both systems, the pirates would have been far less successful on their voyages. Similarly, we need to know that we have two systems built into our brains for a reason, and we should know how and when to use both. Your gut is a powerful decision making tool but should only be trusted when it is founded in experience. Statistics, like oars are far less fun to use but they get results. Learn to use them both and often in conjunction. As Daniel Kahneman, the Nobel Prize-winning economist said, "think fast and slow."

Part 2: The Points of Sail

Selling, much like sailing, requires tactile navigation. Even when you have mapped out your course perfectly, there will always snags and driftwood, storms and rough seas. Open with honesty, transparency, and empathy and your customers will be more likely to navigate that with you. Challenge their perspectives and bring new ones to light. Anchor your value to the why and cast a vision for the future. Walk the plank with them, and even let them win at times. Just know the 20 percent you aren't willing to give up. Lastly, set measurements and metrics for success. The "asks" need to be specific and allow for a future path and additional voyages. Remember sustainability thrives and dies with the lifetime customer, and the "why" will always lead the way to "*buy!*"

Pirate Tips and Notes

Tip #1 Get Organized

Don't underestimate the power of getting organized. Use down time to research and pick an ecosystem like google where you can tie all your calendars, notes, email, file share, and contacts together. This way everything is stored in one place and you can add new tools to your arsenal more quickly because you're familiar with how the ecosystem works. Google calendar, work email tied to a Gmail account, Google Drive, Google Sheets, and even Google Analytics are all powerful tools.

Tip #2 Brand Yourself

Brand yourself. Hone in on the strengths that are unique to you and that resonate with your internal and external customer base to help focus your energy. What works for powerful brands like Apple and Budweiser, works for people. What do you think of when you hear about Elon Musk, Steve Jobs, or even Donald Trump in the news? Could you not describe in three words their brand? Like them or not, their brand works for their target audience.

Tip #3 Anchor in the Why

Understand the customer's "why" and you will guide them to "buy". Think in terms of the BMW car sale. BMW's are known for their engines. However, if you spend your entire sales pitch talking about the engine when the customer wants it as a status symbol then you've at the very least wasted time. Start with uncovering the why and then tailor the pitch around it.

Tip #4 Prepare to Win a Million Dollars

Make preparation and research what sets you apart. Be reminded of the analogy made to interview prep. If someone offered you a million dollars to beat out five other people on a presentation next

Friday how would you prepare to be assured your pitch wins? Good new sales jobs and big customer prospects often have this kind of valuation or more over time. Prepare in a way that assures you will beat out the other five presentations.

Tip #5 Don't Break the Law!

Pareto's Law that is. 80% of output will come from the top 20% of input. What are your most important 20% of customer targets? What 20% of things drive 80% of your outcomes? Find the most important things and place your focus here. When you get close to execution then use the Cannonball Approach and go all in. Don't be afraid to crash or miss on a few. It will happen.

Tip #6 Embrace Crashes and Misses

Embrace the crashes and misses. Those that have mastered anything failed a lot along the way. The difference is that they learn quickly from the mistakes and apply the learnings. Look at failure as future opportunity and don't spend too much time making excuses or benchmarking the failure to others.

Tip #7 Use Both Your Decision-Making Systems

Use both your sails and oars when making decisions. We were born with two decision making systems and they work best when we use them both. Think of your sail as your gut or experience and thus the immediate thought or reaction. Think of the oars as the slow and analytical decision-making system. Combine weighted algorithms and analytics with experience and gut reaction when making important decisions.

Tip #8 Win the First Five Seconds

Open sales calls with the goal of winning over the customer in the first five seconds. These are the most important five seconds of the sales call because if it doesn't win you more time your toast. Open with a goal of building immediate trust. Empathy, transparency, and at times brutal honesty will help guide the way.

Tip #9 Build Belief with a Visual

Studies show your recall is 68% percent better three days post learning something new when it's tied to a visual. More alarming is that 90% of what you hear is forgotten without one.

Tip # 10 Frame Loss not Gain

One of the top 3 behavior change tactics is to frame the loss. What will be lost by not changing something will often have more impact than what is to be gained. Reference Tip 9. Was this this case for you?

Tip #11 Negotiation is Not about Winning an Argument

According to Top FBI negotiators, winning should not be the goal of a negotiation. Instead set a goal of mutually beneficial terms and try to get the other party to say, "that's right." Prepare more than you pitch and try your best to understand all the potential "black swans" that in hindsight killed negotiations in the past.

Tip # 12 Three Questions to Ask Before Making a Goal

Can this be achieved? Does this need to be achieved above other things? Can I COMMIT to achieving it? Commitments are much different than loosely defined goals for success. Don't waste time on something new if you aren't committed to it.

Tip # 13 Downtime on the Dead Seas?

If you find yourself in a slow period or find some dead air in your day then do something that will improve not diffuse you. If a sales appointment you were excited about cancels, or you just have hit a dry spell, then don't panic. Know this time was coming, grant yourself it, and have a plan for productive things to do during it.

Tip # 14 Adjustments to Make for a Better Start

Read the Miracle Morning by Hal Elrod and develop a morning routine that gets you off to a great start to your day.

Tip #15 Influence

When trying to create influence, turn to the laws of reciprocity, scarcity, and the need for consensus.

Tip #16 Announce your Stretch Goals

If you have set a stretch goal, and you are ready to commit to it, then start telling a few people about it. Once you have told others you will start to belief and feel a sense of ownership in achieving it.

Tip # 17 Waving White Flags- Your Low Hanging Fruit.

Pay attention to changes in the market or customer's organization as this often spells opportunity. Any new business or order that seemingly pops onto your sales dashboard is worth investigating for this reason. Also, rural communities, or cities on the outskirts of your geography often have less competition and are good starting points.

Tip # 18 Go to the Gemba

The gemba is where the action takes place. Learn your customers business prior to trying to help them. Entrench yourself on the opportunities with the highest potential for return on investment.

Tip #19 Elicit Emotion

Emotions create connections and connections create sales. What emotion does your product create? Happiness? Safety? Status? Find the emotions that fit with your product and try to fold and weave them into your messaging.

Tip # 20 Target with a Cannonball not a Shotgun

In order to sink a big ship and close a big deal you have to avoid all fear and go all in. Know when one is in your sights and go get it.

Tip #21 Deliver V.A.L.U.E

Variability: Where there is variability of product, service, or outcome, there is an opportunity to help the customer. **A**utomation: Look for areas you can help the customer alleviate manual or redundant tasks. **L**ower Cost: You can reduce cost a number of ways for customers without lowering prices. **U**niquely Different: How can your product or service uniquely differentiate your customer. **E**xcess Waste: How can you eliminate waste of time, money, or talent for the customer.

Tip #22 Use Trusted Sources

Find and develop a short list of references that will validate and even sell for you. A trusted source alleviates concern and fear for the customer.

Tip #23 Earn the Right to Close

Closing is not what the movies depict. You have to earn the right to close. You'll know when you really have it down when you feel confident telling the customer the next steps instead of asking. If you're telling them the next steps and they are hesitant then you have missed the anchor and you need to circle back.

Tip #24 Metrics and Measurement

Remember the January 1st gym analogy? Trainers succeed in getting more people to stick to their goals by using more than just a scale. What measurements are most important to your customer? How can you track it? Create your KPI's from this list and consistently and routinely present on these measurements.

Tip #25 Be a Pirate

Go out and find those that already seemingly mastered what your trying to achieve and learn from them! As Steve Jobs said, "It's more fun to be a pirate than join the Navy."

Goal Setting Worksheet

List Your Top Five Stretch Goals:

_____	1. Y N 2. Y N 3. Y N
_____	1. Y N 2. Y N 3. Y N
_____	1. Y N 2. Y N 3. Y N
_____	1. Y N 2. Y N 3. Y N
_____	1. Y N 2. Y N 3. Y N

Ask Yourself These Three Questions for Each of Your Stretch Goals:

1. Can this realistically be achieved?
2. Does this need to be achieved above other things?
3. Can I COMMIT to achieving this?

Define Your Stretch Goal Here:

_____

_____

_____

Define Your S.M.A.R.T Goals (your waypoints along the way to your stretch goal) **for the first 30, 60, 90 Days:** _____

_____

_____

_____

List All Tools or Resources You Will Need to Help Guide You:

_____

_____

_____

SELF-BRANDING WORKSHEET

TAKE THE FREE COLORS/DISC ASSESSMENT AT
discpersonalitytesting.com/free-disc-test/

LIST WORDS THAT DESCRIBE YOUR PERSONALITY TRAITS CURRENTLY ALONG WITH TRAITS THAT WILL DIFFERENTIATE YOU UNIQUELY:

_____

_____

_____

_____

LIST THREE WORDS THAT DESCRIBE YOUR BRAND BEST:

_____ _____ _____

TAGLINE OR MOTTO:

_____

FEEDBACK CHALLENGE:

EMAIL 10-15 CLOSE FAMILY, FRIENDS, OR COLLEAGUES FOR FEEDBACK. EXPLAIN THAT YOU ARE TRYING TO UNDERSTAND YOUR PERSONAL STRENGTHS AND WEAKNESSES. EXPLAIN THAT THEY ARE A TRUSTED SOURCE TO YOU AND THAT THEIR FEEDBACK IS IMPORTANT AS YOU TRY TO UNDERSTAND AREAS TO FOCUS ON FOR IMPROVEMENT.

LIST FEEDBACK BELOW:

_____

_____

_____

BIBLIOGRAPHY

"The Brain-Gut Connection." *Johns Hopkins Medicine*, www.hopkinsmedicine.org/health/wellness-and-prevention/the-brain-gut-connection.

Carnegie, Dorothy. *How to Win Friends and Influence People*. Simon & Schuster, 1981.

Carney, Scott. *What Doesn't Kill Us*. Scribe Publications, 2019.

Cialdini, Robert B. *Influence: the Psychology of Persuasion: Robert B. Cialdini*. Collins, 2007.

Dalio, Ray. *Principles*. Simon and Schuster, 2017.

Dennis, Pascal. *Lean Production Simplified: a Plain-Language Guide to the World's Most Powerful Production System*. CRC Press, Taylor & Francis Group, 2017.

Dickens, Charles. *A Christmas Carol*. Madison Market Ltd., 1989.

Dixon, Matthew, and Brent Adamson. *The Challenger Sale: Taking Control of the Customer Conversation*. Portfolio Penguin, 2013.

Duhigg, Charles. *Smarter Faster Better: the Secrets of Being Productive in Life and Business*. Random House, 2017.

Duhigg, Charles. *The Power of Habit: Why We Do What We Do and How to Change*. Random House, 2013.

Durant, Will, and Ariel Durant. *The Lessons of History by Will and Ariel Durant*. Simon and Schuster, 1968.

"Forbes.com Quotes Steve Jobs Quote ." *Forbes*, Forbes Magazine, 2019, www.forbes.com/quotes/11376/. Quote "It's More Fun to Be a Pirate Than Join the Navy"-Steve Jobs

"Free DISC Test." *DISC Personality Testing*, discpersonalitytesting.com/free-disc-test/.

Graser, Marc. "Epic Fail: How Blockbuster Could Have Owned Netflix." *Variety*, 8 Dec. 2013, variety.com/2013/biz/news/epic-fail-how-blockbuster-could-have-owned-netflix-1200823443/.

Heath, Chip, and Dan Heath. *Made to Stick: Why Some Ideas Survive and Others Die*. Random House Books, 2010.

"The History and Evolution of SMART Goals." *AchieveIt*, 3 July 2018, www.achieveit.com/resources/blog/the-history-and-evolution-of-smart-goals.

Horsley, Kevin. "Unlimited Memory: How to Use Advanced Learning Strategies to Learn Faster, Remember More and Be More Productive." *Unlimited Memory: How to Use Advanced Learning Strategies to Learn Faster, Remember More and Be More Productive*, TCK Publishing, 2016, pp. 1–5.

"The Invisible Gorilla Harvard Experiment." *The Invisible Gorilla: And Other Ways Our Intuitions Deceive Us*, 2010, www.theinvisiblegorilla.com/gorilla_experiment.html.

Kahneman, Daniel. *Thinking, Fast and Slow*. Farrar, Straus and Giroux, 2015.

Lavinsky, Dave. "The Two Most Important Quotes In Business." *Growthink*, 13 Sept. 2019, www.growthink.com/content/two-most-important-quotes-business.

MANSON, MARK. *SUBTLE ART OF NOT GIVING A F*CK: a Counterintuitive Approach to Living a Good Life.* NEWBURY House Publishers, 2019.

Moynihan, Tim. "Google's Year in Search Is Back and Better Than Ever." *Wired*, Conde Nast, 3 June 2017, www.wired.com/2015/12/googles-year-in-search-is-more-interactive-and-granular-than-ever/.

Navarro, Joe, and Marvin Karlins. *What Every BODY Is Saying: an Ex-FBI Agent's Guide to Speed-Reading People.* Harper Collins, 2015.

"The Power of Communication: Helen Keller." *TeamBonding*, 5 June 2018, www.teambonding.com/power-of-communication/.

PowerfulJRE. "Joe Rogan Experience #1212 - David Goggins." *YouTube*, YouTube, 5 Dec. 2018, www.youtube.com/watch?v=BvWB7B8tXK8.

PowerfulJRE. "Joe Rogan Experience #712 - Wim Hof." *YouTube*, YouTube, 21 Oct. 2015, www.youtube.com/watch?v=Np0jGp6442A.

"Prospect Theory: Behavioraleconomics.com: The BE Hub." *Behavioraleconomics.com | The BE Hub*, 26 Aug. 2019, www.behavioraleconomics.com/resources/mini-encyclopedia-of-be/prospect-theory/.

Shankman, Peter. *Faster than Normal: Turbocharge Your Focus, Productivity, and Success with the Secrets of the ADHD Brain.* TarcherPerigee, an Imprint of Penguin Random House LLC, 2017.

Simpson, Sturgill. "Sturgill Simpson – Voices." *Genius*, genius.com/Sturgill-simpson-voices-lyrics.

Talks, TEDx. "Three Myths of Behavior Change - What You Think You Know That You Don't: Jeni Cross at TEDxCSU." *YouTube*, YouTube, 20 Mar. 2013, www.youtube.com/watch?v=l5d8GW6GdR0.

TED. "How Great Leaders Inspire Action | Simon Sinek." *YouTube*, YouTube, 4 May 2010, www.youtube.com/watch?v=qp0HIF3SfI4.

"Understanding the Pareto Principle (The 80/20 Rule)." *BetterExplained*, betterexplained.com/articles/understanding-the-pareto-principle-the-8020-rule/.

The V Foundation for Cancer Research, V Foundation for Cancer Research. "Jim's 1993 ESPY Speech." *YouTube*, YouTube, 28 Sept. 2008, www.youtube.com/watch?v=HuoVM9nm42E.

Vance, Ashlee. *Elon Musk: How the Billionaire CEO of SpaceX and Tesla Is Shaping Our Future*. Virgin Books, 2015.

Voss, Christopher, and Tahl Raz. *Never Split the Difference: Negotiating as If Your Life Depended on It*. RH Business Books, 2016.

Womack, James P., and Daniel T. Jones. *Lean Thinking: Banish Waste and Create Wealth in Your Corporation*. Free Press, 2010.

THE

END

.

ABOUT THE AUTHOR

Our backgrounds shape us all, and I've been blessed with a unique blend of experiences. I grew up on a farm, and my mother's side of the family was blue collar, while my father's side was all doctors, surgeons, and nurses. These family structures might seem different on the surface, but hard work, perseverance, and creativity ran deep throughout. Today, I'm a top performing "sales guy" in the medical field, and my passion and drive are built upon the very foundation of that upbringing.

It hasn't always been easy, though. Having spent most of my life coping with undiagnosed ADHD, learning was always a challenge. However, as I grew older, I learned more about how to use these gifts. I was hungry for knowledge and wanted to take in everything I could get my hands on. You could say I've become a hyper-learner, and writing has become my way to sharpen the tools I've worked so hard to obtain. Now it's time to share those tools. It's my sincere hope that this book connected with both your heart and mind.

Made in the USA
San Bernardino, CA
15 March 2020